数量表現の英語トレーニングブック

Practical Manual: Quantitative Expressions in English

Sakurako Oshima 大島さくら子 [著]

［CD2枚付］

はじめに

　初級から上級レベルのすべての英語学習者にとって、英語の数量表現は通常とても難しいものです。英文をすらすら読んだり、英語をスムーズに話したり、何の不都合もなく聞いていても、数字の箇所では思考が止まってしまうという経験を、多くの方がされているのではないでしょうか。

　英語の数字を苦手とする背景には、まず、英語の数字を読む際、日本語と桁の区切りが違うため読みにくいというのがあります。住所の番地や電話番号などの区切り方や読み方も、日本語の数字と違います。また、使用されている通貨や、メートル法、ヤード・ポンド法などの単位系が、国によって異なります。ですから、このような背景やルールを知らないと、正確に読んで話し、そして聞き取ることがなかなかできないのです。

　本書では、新聞、雑誌などの文章、ビジネスや日常での会話の中に出てくるさまざまな数量表現を、どう読み、聞き、話すのかを、豊富な例文で紹介しています。そして、付属のCDには、これらの数量表現を含む、たくさんのトレーニング問題が、ネィティブスピーカーによってナチュラルスピードで録音されています。これらを徹底的に聞き込み、問題を繰り返し解くことによって、数字に慣れ、強くなっていくことができます。

　また、付録として、センチメートルをフィートに、キロメートルをマイルに、そして華氏を摂氏に換算する換算式と、演習問題を載せました。さらに、海外旅行や出張で、レストランで食事をしたり、タクシーに乗ったりしてチップを支払う際、支払額を見て即座に、15～20％のチップをどのように計算するのかのヒントも載せてあります。

　皆さんにとって本書が、英語の数量表現を日本語と同じくらいの理解度とスピードで、自由に操ることができるようになるための、一助になれば幸いです。

　　　　　　　　　　　　　　　　　　　　　　　　　　　大島さくら子

本書の使い方と特徴

《トレーニング問題の種類》

1　CD から流れてくる英文の数字を聴き、書き取る、穴埋め問題。

＊中～上級レベルの学習者は、流れてくる英文を聴きながら（あるいは解答の英文を読みながら）、さらに和訳を出してみてください。

2　CD から流れてくる日本語（数字と単位などを含むフレーズ、短い文）を聴き、即座に英語に直して発話する、簡単な通訳演習問題。

＊メモを取りながら、解答した後、解答文と CD に録音されている音声でチェックしてください。

＊どうしても音声だけでは難しい場合は、解答欄の日本語を見ながら解答してください。

3　数字を含む日本語を、英語に直して発話する英作文問題。

＊１問ずつ、解答文と CD に録音されている音声で、自分の解答をチェックしてください。

＊文が長過ぎる、あるいは発話した英語の記憶が無くなるなど、自分の解答が正しいかどうか正確に確認できない場合は、英語を書き出してから、解答文と CD に録音されている音声でチェックしてください。

＊ただし、1 の「数字」の 3 は、数字を音読する問題です。

《トレーニング問題数》

1……合計 354 問
2……合計 204 問
3……合計 184 問

　　＊問題数は各項目で異なります。次ページの表 1 を、参照してください。

《発音とアクセント》
CD の音声は、アメリカ人男性とカナダ人女性によって録音されていますので、発音とアクセントはアメリカ／カナダ英語です。

《アメリカ英語とイギリス英語》
本書を通して、アメリカ英語とイギリス英語が混在しています。また、数字の表記の仕方や読み方は、同じアメリカ英語、イギリス英語の中にも何種類かありますので、本書ではあえて 1 つに統一せずに、日常でさまざまに使われているものをそのまま載せています。

[表1]

1	：徹底トレーニング	1 10〜15問	2 10問	3 5問
2、3、8	：徹底トレーニング（Step 1）	1 5〜10問	2 3〜5問	3 3〜5問
4、5、7	：徹底トレーニング	1 5〜10問	―――	―――
6	：徹底トレーニング	1 10問	2 5問	3 5問
9	：（2、3、8 の）さらなる徹底トレーニング（Step 2）	1 5〜7問	2 3〜5問	3 3〜5問

（注）**6** の「電気器具／設備、カメラ、写真、（その他）」は、1 のみ 10 問です。

CONTENTS

CD BOOK 数量表現の英語トレーニングブック

1 数　字 …………………………………………………… 10

- 基数　　　　　　　　　　　　　　　　　　　　　　10
    1. 基数・徹底トレーニング　　　　　　　　　　　12
- 序数　　　　　　　　　　　　　　　　　　　　　　15
    2. 序数・徹底トレーニング　　　　　　　　　　　17
- 小数　　　　　　　　　　　　　　　　　　　　　　19
    3. 小数・徹底トレーニング　　　　　　　　　　　20
- 分数　　　　　　　　　　　　　　　　　　　　　　22
    4. 分数・徹底トレーニング　　　　　　　　　　　23

2 時間、年齢 ……………………………………………… 26

- 時間　　　　　　　　　　　　　　　　　　　　　　26
    5. 時間・徹底トレーニング Step 1　　　　　　　32
- 年齢　　　　　　　　　　　　　　　　　　　　　　35
    6. 年齢・徹底トレーニング Step 1　　　　　　　38

3 ビジネス、金融、家計 ………………………………… 41

- 通貨、為替　　　　　　　　　　　　　　　　　　　41
    7. 通貨、為替・徹底トレーニング Step 1　　　　46
- 株式、債券　　　　　　　　　　　　　　　　　　　50
    8. 株式、債券・徹底トレーニング Step 1　　　　55
- 売上げ、利益、損益（費用）　　　　　　　　　　　58
    9. 売上げ、利益、損益（費用）・徹底トレーニング Step 1　61
- 料金、価格　　　　　　　　　　　　　　　　　　　65
    10. 料金、価格・徹底 トレーニング Step 1　　　67

- 収入、支出、税金　　　　　　　　　　　　　　　71
    11. 収入、支出、税金・徹底トレーニング Step 1　　76
- ローン、クレジット、金利　　　　　　　　　　　80
    12. ローン、クレジット、金利・徹底トレーニング Step 1　83
- 資産、貯蓄、負債　　　　　　　　　　　　　　　85
    13. 資産、貯蓄、負債・徹底トレーニング Step 1　　87
- 保険、年金　　　　　　　　　　　　　　　　　　89
    14. 保険、年金・徹底トレーニング Step 1　　　　91

4　通信・情報・IT ……………………………………… 93

- 住所、郵便、電話　　　　　　　　　　　　　　　93
- 放送、情報技術　　　　　　　　　　　　　　　　96
- 新聞、雑誌、書籍　　　　　　　　　　　　　　　99
    15. 通信、情報、IT・徹底トレーニング　　　　　101

5　交　通 …………………………………………………… 104

- 飛行機、自動車、電車　　　　　　　　　　　　104
    16. 交通・徹底トレーニング　　　　　　　　　　107

6　日常の数字 …………………………………………… 109

- 食料品、料理　　　　　　　　　　　　　　　　109
    17. 食料品、料理・徹底トレーニング　　　　　　112
- 医療、厚生　　　　　　　　　　　　　　　　　116
    18. 医療、厚生・徹底トレーニング　　　　　　　120
- 電気器具/設備、カメラ、写真　　　　　　　　124
- その他（家族、選挙、法律）　　　　　　　　　127
    19. 電気器具/設備、カメラ、写真、その他（家族、選挙、法律）
        ・徹底トレーニング　　　　　　　　　　　　130

7 教育、文化、スポーツ ……………………………… 133

- 学校、映画、演劇、音楽、スポーツ　　　　　　　　133
    - 20. 教育、文化、スポーツ・徹底トレーニング　　　136
- 衣料品、靴、指輪サイズ一覧　　　　　　　　　　　139

8 単　位 ………………………………………………… 142

- 長さ、幅　　　　　　　　　　　　　　　　　　　142
- その他　　　　　　　　　　　　　　　　　　　　145
    - 21. 長さ、幅・徹底トレーニング Step 1　　　　　147
- 体重、身長 / 体長　　　　　　　　　　　　　　　150
    - 22. 体重、身長 / 体長・徹底トレーニング Step 1　152
- 重さ　　　　　　　　　　　　　　　　　　　　　154
    - 23. 重さ・徹底トレーニング Step 1　　　　　　156
- 深さ / 奥行き、厚さ　　　　　　　　　　　　　　158
    - 24. 深さ / 奥行き、厚さ・徹底トレーニング Step 1　161
- 高さ、高度（標高、海抜）　　　　　　　　　　　163
    - 25. 高さ、高度（標高、海抜）・徹底トレーニング Step 1　166
- 面積、容積 / 体積　　　　　　　　　　　　　　　168
    - 26. 面積、容積 / 体積・徹底トレーニング Step 1　173
- 距離、速度、角度　　　　　　　　　　　　　　　177
    - 27. 距離、速度、角度・徹底トレーニング Step 1　180
- 緯度、経度　　　　　　　　　　　　　　　　　　184
    - 28. 緯度、経度・徹底トレーニング Step 1　　　185
- 気象　　　　　　　　　　　　　　　　　　　　　187
    - 29. 気象・徹底トレーニング Step 1　　　　　　189

9 さらに徹底トレーニング ……………………………… 191

- 30. 時間・徹底トレーニング Step 2　　　　　　　191
- 31. 年齢・徹底トレーニング Step 2　　　　　　　194
- 32. 通貨、為替・徹底トレーニング Step 2　　　　197

33. 株式、債券・徹底トレーニング Step 2　　200
34. 売上げ、利益、損益（費用）・徹底トレーニング Step 2　　203
35. 料金、価格・徹底トレーニング Step 2　　206
36. 収入、支出、税金・徹底トレーニング Step 2　　209
37. ローン、クレジット、金利・徹底トレーニング Step 2　　212
38. 資産、貯蓄、負債・徹底トレーニング Step 2　　215
39. 保険、年金・徹底トレーニング Step 2　　217
40. 長さ、幅・徹底トレーニング Step 2　　220
41. 体重、身長/体長・徹底トレーニング Step 2　　223
42. 重さ・徹底トレーニング Step 2　　226
43. 深さ/奥行き、厚さ・徹底トレーニング Step 2　　229
44. 高さ、高度（標高、海抜）・徹底トレーニング Step 2　　232
45. 面積、容積/体積・徹底トレーニング Step 2　　234
46. 距離、速度、角度・徹底トレーニング Step 2　　237
47. 緯度、経度・徹底トレーニング Step 2　　240
48. 気象・徹底トレーニング Step 2　　242

付録 1 ……… 245
四則演算　　245
数学記号　　246
概数を出す　　246

付録 2 ……… 248
換算演習問題　　248

付録 3 ……… 250
チップの計算方法　　250

1 数 字
Numbers

基数　Cardinal Numbers

基数とは？

　基数は、数量を表すときに用いる基本となる数字です。基数には、偶数（even number）と奇数（odd number）があります。

基数の読み方

　4桁以上の基数は、3桁ごとに区切って読んでいきます。英語には、日本語と違って「万」と「億」を表す単語がないので、桁が大きくなってくると複雑になり、読みにくくなってきます。
　ですから、数字を読むときは、桁の数で単位を把握しておくとよいでしょう。次ページの**表1**でいうと、ゼロ2つが hundred（百）、ゼロ3つが thousand（千）、ゼロ6つが million（百万）、ゼロ9つが billion（十億）、ゼロ12が trillion（兆）になります。

基数の単位

　ten、hundred、thousand、million、billion、trillion は単位ですので、複数形にはなりません。つまり、「三百」は three hundred であり、three hundreds にはなりませんので、注意してください。

不特定多数の表し方

　ただし、不特定の多数を表す際、単位を複数形にして使う表現があります。
- □ hundreds of customers 　　　　　「何百人もの顧客」
- □ thousands of brochures 　　　　　「何千ものパンフレット」
- □ tens of thousands of workers 　　「何万もの労働者」

- hundreds of thousands of dollars 「何十万ドル」
- millions of supporters 「何百万もの支援者」
- tens of millions of low-income families 「何千万組もの低所得家庭」

「数十もの〜、何十もの〜、多数の〜」というときは、tens 〜ではなく dozens of 〜を使います。dozen は「ダース、12個」という意味ですが、きっちり 12 ではなく、通常、12 前後の数を指します。

- dozens of jobs 「何十もの仕事」
- dozens of times 「何十回も、何度も何度も」

[表1]

一	1	one
十	10	ten
百	100	a / one hundred
千	1,000	a / one thousand
一万	10,000	ten thousand
十万	100,000	a / one hundred thousand
百万	1,000,000	a / one million
一千万	10,000,000	ten million
一億	100,000,000	a / one hundred million
十億	1,000,000,000	a / one billion
百億	10,000,000,000	ten billion
一千億	100,000,000,000	a / one hundred billion
一兆	1,000,000,000,000	a / one trillion
十兆	10,000,000,000,000	ten trillion
百兆	100,000,000,000,000	a / one hundred trillion

1 数字

TRACK 1

1 基数・徹底トレーニング

1 CD から流れてくる基数を聴き、書き取ってください。

1)   2)
3)   4)
5)   6)
7)   8)
9)   10)
11)   12)
13)   14)
15)

解答

1)	632	six hundred (and) thirty-two
2)	809	eight hundred (and) nine
3)	3,437	three thousand four hundred (and) thirty-seven
4)	5,600	fifty-six hundred

 ＊このように、five thousand (and) six hundred ではなく、上2桁と下2桁に分ける読み方もあります。ただし、下2桁が00となっている場合に限ります。

5)	756	seven hundred (and) fifty-six
6)	1,710	one thousand seven hundred (and) ten
7)	9,705	nine thousand seven hundred (and) five
8)	468	four hundred (and) sixty-eight
9)	10,020	ten thousand (and) twenty
10)	65,453	sixty-five thousand four hundred (and) fifty-three
11)	57,350	fifty-seven thousand three hundred (and) fifty
12)	40,028	forty thousand (and) twenty-eight
13)	70,836,454	seventy million eight hundred thirty-six thousand four hundred (and) fifty-four
14)	8,927	eight thousand nine hundred (and) twenty-seven
15)	16,239,000	sixteen million two hundred thirty-nine thousand

TRACK 2

2 CDから流れてくる基数を聴き、即座に英語に直して発話してください。（＊日本語の後ポーズがあって、その後すぐに英語が流れます）

1)　　　　　　　　　　2)
3)　　　　　　　　　　4)
5)　　　　　　　　　　6)
7)　　　　　　　　　　8)
9)　　　　　　　　　　10)

1 数字

解 答

1) 27　　　　　　　twenty-seven
2) 42,012　　　　　forty-two thousand (and) twelve
3) 620　　　　　　six hundred (and) twenty
4) 1,058　　　　　one thousand (and) fifty-eight
5) 301　　　　　　three hundred (and) one
6) 197,422　　　　one hundred ninety-seven thousand four hundred (and) twenty-two
7) 1,095,000　　　one million (and) ninety-five thousand
8) 800,008　　　　eight hundred thousand (and) eight
9) 37,260,000　　 thirty-seven million two hundred sixty thousand
10) 1,000,000,000　one billion

3 以下の基数を英語で音読してください。　 **TRACK 3**

1) 937

2) 27,354

3) 3,729

4) 19

5) 5,000

解 答

1) nine hundred (and) thirty-seven
2) twenty-seven thousand three hundred (and) fifty-four
3) three thousand seven hundred (and) twenty-nine
4) nineteen
5) five thousand

序数　Ordinal Numbers

序数とは？

序数は、順番・順序を表すときに用いる数字です。

序数の表し方

1番目、2番目、3番目は決まった語がありますが、4番目以降は基数に th をつけます。原則として、最初に the をつけます。
the 1st (first)、the 2nd (second)、the 3rd (third)、the 4th (fourth)、
the 5th (fifth)、the 6th (sixth)、the 7th (seventh)、... etc.

5番目、9番目、12番目

5番目は fiveth ではなく fifth、9番目は nineth ではなく ninth、12番目は twelveth ではなく twelfth と変則につづります。

21番目から99番目まで

21番目以降99番目までの序数は、10の位を基数で読み、1の位を序数で読みます。つづる際は、10の位と1の位をハイフンでつなぎます。
the 21st (twenty-first)、the 22nd (twenty-second)、
the 23rd (twenty-third)、the 24th (twenty-fourth)、
the 25th (twenty-fifth)、the 26th (twenty-sixth)、...
the 31st (thirty-first)、the 32nd (thirty-second)、... etc.

100番目、200番目、300番目、…の読み方

100番目、200番目、300番目、…は、以下のように読みます。
the 100th (one hundredth)、the 200th (two hundredth)、
the 300th (three hundredth)、the 1,000th (one thousandth)、… etc.

101番目以降

101番目以降も、100の位を基数で読み、1の位を序数で読みますが、つづる際は、ハイフンではなくandでつなぎます。

the 101st (one hundred (and) first)、
the 102nd (one hundred (and) second)、
the 103rd (one hundred (and) third)、
the 104th (one hundred (and) fourth)、… etc.

注意すべき序数

the 20th、the 30th、the 40thなど20以上の2桁数字のうち、1の位がゼロの数字にはそれぞれ、twentieth、thirtieth、fortiethと"e"を入れてつづります。読むときもeを発音します。そのため、the 20th (twentieth) はthe 28th (twenty-eighth) に、the 30th (thirtieth) はthe 38th (thirty-eighth) に聞き間違えることがあります。このように、1の位が8の序数の発音には、特に気をつけましょう。

2 序数・徹底トレーニング

🎧 TRACK 4

1　数字

1 CDから流れてくる序数を聴き、書き取ってください。

1)　　　　　　　　　2)
3)　　　　　　　　　4)
5)　　　　　　　　　6)
7)　　　　　　　　　8)
9)　　　　　　　　　10)

解答

1)　the 12th　　the twelfth
2)　the 49th　　the forty-ninth
3)　the 15th　　the fifteenth
4)　the 30th　　the thirtieth
5)　the 97th　　the ninety-seventh
6)　the 60th　　the sixtieth
7)　the 18th　　the eighteenth
8)　the 26th　　the twenty-sixth
9)　the 70th　　the seventieth
10)　the 11th　　the eleventh

🎧 TRACK 5

2 CDから流れてくる序数を聴き、即座に英語に直して発話してください。（＊日本語の後ポーズがあつて、その後すぐに英語が流れます）

1)　　　　　　　　　2)
3)　　　　　　　　　4)
5)　　　　　　　　　6)
7)　　　　　　　　　8)
9)　　　　　　　　　10)

解答

1)　50回目　　　the 50th　　　the fiftieth

2)	2番目	the 2nd	the second
3)	6回目	the 6th	the sixth
4)	28回目	the 28th	the twenty-eighth
5)	3番目	the 3rd	the third
6)	第101回	the 101st	the one hundred (and) first
7)	2,000回目	the 2,000th	the two thousandth
8)	第312回	the 312th	the three hundred (and) twelfth
9)	1万回目	the 10,000th	the ten thousandth
10)	40万回目	the 400,000th	the four hundred thousandth

3　以下の序数を英語で音読してください。　 TRACK 6

1) the 57th

2) the 10th

3) the 18th

4) the 66th

5) the 20th

解　答

1) the fifty-seventh
2) the tenth
3) the eighteenth
4) the sixty-sixth
5) the twentieth

小数　Decimal Numbers

　小数は、日本語と同じように小数点（decimal point）以下を1つ1つ読んでいきます。小数点以下の数字のゼロは、zero、oh と読みます。1の位の数字がゼロのときは zero か、ゼロを読まずに"点"の point から読み始めます。

- ☐ 1.35　　　　one point three five
- ☐ 0.16　　　　zero point one six、point one six
- ☐ 2.08　　　　two point zero / oh eight
- ☐ 40.95　　　 forty point nine five
- ☐ 300.207　　three hundred point two zero / oh seven

3　小数・徹底トレーニング

🔘 TRACK 7

1　CDから流れてくる小数を聴き、書き取ってください。

1)　　　　　　　　　　2)
3)　　　　　　　　　　4)
5)　　　　　　　　　　6)
7)　　　　　　　　　　8)
9)　　　　　　　　　　10)

[解答]

1)　8.25　　　eight point two five
2)　0.5　　　zero point five
3)　9.321　　nine point three two one
4)　0.007　　point oh oh seven
　　＊1の位の数字がゼロでohと読み、小数点以下にさらにゼロが続くときは、そのままohで読みます。zeroで読むことはあまりありません。
5)　27.49　　twenty-seven point four nine
6)　1.31　　 one point three one
7)　83.3　　 eighty-three point three
8)　5.726　　five point seven two six
9)　0.01　　 zero point zero one
10) 10.72　　ten point seven two

🔘 TRACK 8

2　CDから流れてくる小数を聴き、即座に英語に直して発話してください。（＊日本語の後ポーズがあって、その後すぐに英語が流れます）

1)　　　　　　　　　　2)
3)　　　　　　　　　　4)
5)　　　　　　　　　　6)
7)　　　　　　　　　　8)
9)　　　　　　　　　　10)

解 答

1) 3.02 three point zero / oh two
2) 10.5 ten point five
3) 9.871 nine point eight seven one
4) 0.02 zero point zero two、point zero / oh two
5) 20.36 twenty point three six
6) 300.5 three hundred point five
7) 108.22 one hundred eight point two two
8) 3.00489 three point zero zero four eight nine、
three point oh oh four eight nine
9) 98.101 ninety-eight point one zero / oh one
10) 0.38267 zero point three eight two six seven、
point three eight two six seven

3 以下の小数を英語で音読してください。　TRACK 9

1) 52.39

2) 0.273

3) 60.09

4) 0.1

5) 9.814

解 答

1) fifty-two point three nine
2) zero point two seven three、point two seven three
3) sixty point zero / oh nine
4) zero point one、point one
5) nine point eight one four

分数　Fractional Numbers

　分数は、分子（numerator）を基数、分母（denominator）を序数で読みます。そして、日本語と反対に、分子から先に読んでいきます。ただし、2 分の 1 の分母は second ではなく half を使い、4 分の 1 の分母は quarter と fourth のいずれかを使います。分子が 2 以上の場合、分母は複数形になるので、注意してください。
　表記の仕方は、分子と分母の数字の間に、通常、ハイフンを置きますが、省略しても問題ありません。特に、分子が a と one のときは、ほとんどの場合省略されます。

☐ $\frac{1}{2}$　　（a half、one half）

☐ $\frac{1}{4}$　　（a quarter、one quarter、a fourth、one fourth）

☐ $\frac{1}{3}$　　（a third、one third）

☐ $\frac{2}{3}$　　（two-thirds）

☐ $\frac{3}{4}$　　（three-quarters、three-fourths）

☐ $5\frac{4}{7}$　　（five and four-sevenths）

☐ $\frac{285}{1,647}$　　（two hundred (and) eighty-five over one thousand six hundred (and) forty-seven）

　　＊数字が大きく複雑な場合は、分子も分母も基数で読み、「〜分の」にあたる部分を over で表します。

☐ $\frac{1}{100}$　　（one hundredth）

　　＊これは、one one hundredth にはなりません。$\frac{1}{1000}$ も one thousandth となり、同様に分母の序数の one を省略します。

☐ $1\frac{1}{2}$ hours　　（one and a half hours）

☐ $\frac{2}{3}$ mile　　（two-thirds of a mile）

4 分数・徹底トレーニング

TRACK 10

1 CD から流れてくる分数を聴き、書き取ってください。

1) 2)
3) 4)
5) 6)
7) 8)
9) 10)

解 答

1) $\dfrac{5}{8}$ five-eighths

2) $1\dfrac{1}{2}$ one and a half

3) $\dfrac{2}{3}$ two-thirds

4) $\dfrac{3}{5}$ three-fifths

5) $\dfrac{1}{4}$ a quarter

6) $7\dfrac{2}{9}$ seven and two-ninths

7) $\dfrac{1}{5}$ a fifth

8) $4\dfrac{4}{7}$ four and four-sevenths

9) $\dfrac{1}{100}$ one hundredth

10) $\dfrac{12}{179}$ twelve over one hundred (and) seventy-nine

TRACK 11

2 CDから流れてくる分数を聴き、即座に英語に直して発話してください。（＊日本語の後ポーズがあって、その後すぐに英語が流れます）

1) 　　　　　　　　　2)
3) 　　　　　　　　　4)
5) 　　　　　　　　　6)
7) 　　　　　　　　　8)
9) 　　　　　　　　　10)

解　答

1)　6分の5　　　$\dfrac{5}{6}$　　　five-sixths

2)　2と3分の1　　$2\dfrac{1}{3}$　　two and a third

3)　10分の1　　　$\dfrac{1}{10}$　　one tenth

4)　3分の2　　　$\dfrac{2}{3}$　　　two-thirds

5)　1と4分の3　　$1\dfrac{3}{4}$　　one and three-quarters、one and three-fourths

6)　40分の7　　　$\dfrac{7}{40}$　　seven over forty、seven-fortieths

7)　100万分の1　　$\dfrac{1}{1,000,000}$　one over a million、one millionth

8)　1,000分の1　　$\dfrac{1}{1,000}$　one thousandth

9)　1万分の9　　　$\dfrac{9}{10,000}$　nine over ten thousands、nine-ten thousandths

10)　100分の53　　$\dfrac{53}{100}$　fifty-three over one hundred、fifty-three hundredths

3 以下の分数を英語で音読してください。　　🎧 TRACK 12

1) $\dfrac{4}{9}$

2) $3\dfrac{1}{4}$

3) $\dfrac{7}{8}$

4) $57\dfrac{1}{2}$

5) $\dfrac{167}{982}$

解答

1) four-ninths
2) three and a / one quarter、three and a / one fourth
3) seven-eighths
4) fifty-seven and a half
5) one hundred (and) sixty-seven over nine hundred (and) eighty-two

2 時間、年齢
Time、Age

時間 Time

時刻

～時～分

- 9:05 (nine oh five、five past / after nine)
  [9時5分、9時5分過ぎ]
- 3:17 (three seventeen、seventeen past / after three)
  [3時17分、3時17分過ぎ]
- 5:30 (five thirty、(a) half past five)
  [5時半、5時30分過ぎ]
- 12:15 (twelve fifteen、(a) quarter past / after twelve)
  [12時15分、12時15分過ぎ]
- 1:45 (one forty-five、(a) quarter to / before / of two)
  [1時45分、2時15分前]
- 8:40 (eight forty、twenty to / before / of nine)
  [8時40分、9時20分前]

午前（に）

- You can still see people in the street at 2 or 3 <u>a.m.</u> / two or three <u>in the morning</u>.
  [午前2時や3時に、通りにまだ人がいるのがわかる]

午後（に）

- I made an appointment with the dentist at 4:00 <u>p.m.</u> / four <u>in the afternoon</u>.
  [私は午後4時に、歯医者の予約を入れた]

正午(に)

- [ ] The event takes place from 9:00 a.m. to noon.
  [そのイベントは、午前9時から正午までおこなわれる]
- [ ] The verdict is expected at midday / noon.
  [評決は、正午に出されることになっている]

夕方(に)

- [ ] The main gate will be closed by 7:00 in the evening.
  [正門は、夕方7時までに閉まる]

夜(に)

- [ ] We finished filming at 9:00 at night.
  [私たちは、夜9時に撮影を終了した]

午前零時、真夜中(に)

- [ ] Militants attacked the city, starting just after midnight.
  [過激派は、午前零時をちょうど過ぎたとき、その都市を襲った]
- [ ] Twenty people were forced to flee their homes in the middle of the night.
  [20名の人々が、真夜中に家から逃げ出さなければならなかった]

時、分、秒

～時間、～分、～秒

- [ ] He finished in 2 hours 6 minutes and 25 seconds to win the Chicago Marathon.
  [シカゴマラソンで、彼は2時間6分25秒のタイムで優勝した]

30 秒

☐ Add the red wine, letting it boil for about half a minute.
　［赤ワインを加え、約 30 秒煮る］

30 分

☐ This news show brings you world news every half-hour.
　［この報道番組は、30 分ごとに世界のニュースを視聴者に届ける］
☐ The bad weather returned half an hour later.
　［30 分後に、また悪天候となった］

15 分

☐ She spoke to me on the phone for about a quarter of an hour.
　［彼女は、電話で約 15 分間、私にしゃべった］

45 分

☐ The police didn't show up for three-quarters of an hour.
　［警察は、45 分現れなかった］

〜時間半

☐ The tour lasts approximately one and a half hours / an hour and a half.
　［そのツアーは、約 1 時間半かかる］

〜分 15 秒

☐ Each course takes around one and a quarter minutes.
　［それぞれの行程は、約 1 分 15 秒かかる］

2 時間、年齢

～秒 / 分 / 時間の

☐ The game was shown with a five-second delay on TV.
　［その試合は、テレビでは 5 秒遅れだった］
☐ To hear the full 10-minute interview, click on the audio link on this page.
　［10 分間の完全インタビューを聞くには、このページのオーディオリンクをクリックする］
☐ They had a three-hour meeting on the issue.
　［彼らはその問題に関して、3 時間の話し合いをした］

24 時間の

☐ The patrol is in force around the clock / round-the-clock.
　［パトロールは、24 時間体制で実施中である］
☐ He was hired as a security guard at the 24 / 7 Call Center.
　［彼は 24 時間、年中無休のコールセンターに、警備員として雇われた］
　＊ 24 / 7 には「いつも（四六時中）、しょっちゅう、常に」という意味もあります。
　＊ 24-7 とも書きます。読み方は、twenty-four seven です。

月日、西暦

～月、～日

☐ January 21　　(January twenty-first)
☐ 21 January　　(the twenty-first of January)
　［1 月 21 日］

～年、～月、～日

☐ March 4, 1965　　(March fourth, nineteen sixty-five)
☐ 4 March 1965　　(the fourth of March nineteen sixty-five)
　［1965 年 3 月 4 日］

～年

- ☐ 1870　　（eighteen seventy）
- ☐ 1900　　（nineteen hundred）
- ☐ 1903　　（nineteen oh three）
- ☐ 2000　　（two thousand）
- ☐ 2001　　（two thousand（and）one）
- ☐ 493　　（four hundred（and）ninety-three、four nine three）
- ☐ 706　　（seven oh six、seven hundred and six）

～年、～月、～日に

- ☐ in 2009　　（in two thousand and nine）
  [2009年に]
- ☐ in June
  [6月に]
- ☐ on May 10　　（on May tenth）
  [5月10日に]

世紀、年号、～代

紀元（西暦）/ 紀元前

- ☐ A.D. / AD 810、810 A.D. / AD
  [紀元（西暦）810年]
  - ＊A.D. は、ラテン語の *Anno Domini* の略です。省略符を用いず AD とも書きます。
  - ＊A.D. は、年号の前と後ろの、どちらにも置けます。
  - ＊A.D. を英語で説明する場合は、in the year of (the / Our) Lord、あるいは Christian Era といいます。
- ☐ 500 B.C. / BC
  [紀元前500年]
  - ＊B.C. は、before Christ の略です。省略符を用いず BC とも書きます。
  - ＊B.C. は、必ず年号の後ろに置きます。

～世紀

- the 19th century（the nineteenth century）
  [19世紀]
- the 20th century（the twentieth century）
  [20世紀]
- the 21st century（the twenty-first century）
  [21世紀]
- a / one century
  [1世紀]
- half a century、five decades
  [半世紀]
- a quarter of a century、a quarter century
  [四半世紀]

年号、～年代

- the 21st year of the Heisei Era / Period
  [平成21年]
- the first decade of the Showa Era / Period
  [昭和一桁]
- in the 1970s、in the nineteen seventies
  [1970年代に]
- in the early 1800s、in the early eighteen hundreds
  [1800年代初頭に]
- in the mid-60s、in the mid-sixties
  [60年代の中ごろに]
- in the late 1980s、in the late nineteen eighties
  [1980年代後半に]

5 時間・徹底トレーニング Step 1

TRACK 13

1 CD から流れてくる英文を聴き、カッコの部分を書き取ってください。

1) The explosion occurred shortly after (　　) a.m. on June (　　), (　　).

2) At the museum's Archaeology Zone, there are (　　) century Turkish costumes that you can try on.

3) Rooms will be available from July (　　), and reservations are now being taken.

4) The first round-table discussion will be held on the weekend of September (　　).

5) It detected a severe, (　　)-minute disturbance on (　　) August.

6) A couple of years ago, we had a chance to make some short (　　)-minute dramas.

7) Information on traffic delays and construction is updated (　　).

8) Born in the (　　) century, she was no ordinary nun.

9) My journey to the island involved a bus journey of (　　) hours and then a (　　)-hour ferry crossing.

10) In (　　) BC, Egypt became embroiled in the conflict in Rome between Julius Caesar and Pompey.

解答

1) The explosion occurred shortly after (7) a.m. on June (30), (1908).
　　[1908年6月30日の午前7時ちょっと過ぎに、爆発が起こった]

2) At the museum's Archaeology Zone, there are (19th) century Turkish costumes that you can try on.
[博物館の考古学ゾーンでは、19世紀のトルコ民族衣装の試着ができる]

3) Rooms will be available from July (11), and reservations are now being taken.
[客室は7月11日より利用可能、現在予約受け付け中]

4) The first round-table discussion will be held on the weekend of September (9).
[第1回の座談会は、9月9日の週末に開かれる]

5) It detected a severe, (five)-minute disturbance on (27) August.
[8月27日に、深刻な5分間の妨害を感知した]

6) A couple of years ago, we had a chance to make some short (ten)-minute dramas.
[2〜3年前に私たちは、10分間の短いドラマをいくつか制作するチャンスがあった]

7) Information on traffic delays and construction is updated (24-7).
[交通の遅延と道路工事の情報は、常に更新される]

8) Born in the (16th) century, she was no ordinary nun.
[彼女は16世紀に生まれ、決して平凡な修道女ではなかった]

9) My journey to the island involved a bus journey of (two) hours and then a (three)-hour ferry crossing.
[私がその島へ行くのに、2時間バスに乗り、その後フェリーで3時間かかった]

10) In (48) BC, Egypt became embroiled in the conflict in Rome between Julius Caesar and Pompey.
[紀元前48年、エジプトは、ローマでのシーザーとポンペイウスの争いに巻き込まれた]

TRACK 14

2 CDから流れてくる日本語を聴き、即座に英語に直して発話してください。(＊日本語の後ポーズがあって、その後すぐに英語が流れます)

1)   2)
3)   4)
5)

解　答

1)　3 時間 26 分　　　　　3 hours and 26 minutes
2)　1900 年代に　　　　　in the 1900s
3)　21 世紀　　　　　　　the 21st Century
4)　午後 5 時半　　　　　5:30 p.m.（five thirty、(a) half past five）
5)　紀元前 840 年　　　　840 BC

3　以下の日本語を英語に直して発話してください。　🄪 TRACK 15

1)　テクノロジーが、50 年代半ばに導入された。

2)　日出：午前 6 時 40 分、日入：午後 7 時 33 分

3)　次回のキッズプログラムは、3 月 8 日に開催される。

4)　それは、1960 年代初頭に盗まれた。

5)　私は、約 5 時間の睡眠をとった。

解　答

1)　Technology arrived in the mid-50s.
2)　Sunrise: 6:40 A.M., Sunset: 7:33 P.M.
3)　The next kids' program will be held March 8.
4)　It was stolen in the early 1960s.
5)　I got around 5 hours of sleep.

年齢　Age

～歳　　～ years old、～ -year-old、age(s) ～、aged ～

- They interviewed 30 children from 5 to 11 years old.
  ［彼らは、5～11歳までの30人の子どもたちに、インタビューをした］
- George, a soft-spoken 41-year-old, is a sales representative.
  ［ジョージは、穏やかな話し方をする41歳の販売員だ］
- Katie, age 9, is enjoying an outing with her mother.
  ［ケイティは、9歳、母親とのお出かけを楽しんでいる］
- A woman, aged 26, and a man, aged 35, were arrested on the suspicion of theft.
  ［女性26歳、男性35歳が、窃盗の容疑で逮捕された］

～歳で、～歳のとき　　at the age of ～、at age ～、at ～

- He got remarried at the age of 54.
  ［彼は、54歳で再婚した］
- At age seven, he and his whole family moved to France.
  ［7歳のとき、彼と彼の家族全員がフランスへ移住した］
- At 27, she was selected as the editor-in-chief.
  ［27歳で、彼女は編集長に抜擢された］

～代　　in one's ～s、～s

- Trained men and women in their twenties are scarce.
  ［訓練を受けた20代の男女が、不足している］
- I am entering my 30s.
  ［私は、もうすぐ30代だ］
- The biggest shift has been among young teens.
  ［最も大きな変化は、10代の若者たちの間で見られた］
  ＊ teenager / teens は13～19歳までを表します。

～代前半 / 半ば / 後半　　in one's early / mid / late ～

☐ The criminal was in his early 20s, about 170 cm and of medium build.
　［犯人は20代前半で、身長約170 cm、中肉中背だった］
☐ When I first started driving around America, I was in my mid-fifties.
　［私が最初にアメリカを車で旅し始めたとき、私は50代の半ばだった］
☐ She looked in her late sixties.
　［彼女は、60代後半に見えた］

年齢層　　age group、age bracket

☐ My parents made friends in all age groups.
　［私の両親は、あらゆる年齢層の人たちと友達になった］
☐ The percentage of women in that age bracket with one child was 9.6 percent.
　［その年齢層で、子どもを1人持つ女性の割合は9.6%だった］

～歳以上　　～ and / or older、over ～

☐ Less than 2 percent of women who are 80 and older die of breast cancer.
　［80歳以上の女性の2%未満が、乳がんで亡くなっている］
☐ I don't think everybody over 30 is over the hill.
　［私は30歳以上の人のすべてが、最盛期を過ぎているわけではないと思う］

～歳以下　　～ and / or younger

☐ Hyde Park, Daily, 9 a.m. to 5 p.m.; $14, free for 15 and younger.
　［ハイドパーク、毎日、午前9時から午後5時まで開園；入園料14ドル、15歳以下は無料］

～歳未満　　under / below age ～、under / below ～

☐ That question was asked in an informal survey of passengers <u>below age 12</u>.
　［その質問は、<u>12 歳未満</u>の乗客に対する、非公式の調査の中においてなされた］

その他

☐ at an early age　　　　　　　幼時に、幼い頃に、若年時に
☐ at a young / younger age　　　若くして
☐ at an older age、in old age　　高齢で、年を取って
☐ between the ages of ～ and …　～歳から…歳の / で / のとき
☐ aged ～ to …　　　　　　　　～歳から…歳（で）

6 年齢・徹底トレーニング Step 1

TRACK 16

1 CD から流れてくる英文を聴き、カッコの部分を書き取ってください。

1) Tributes are paid to the former bishop who died at the age of (　　) after a long illness.

2) He said it is an offense to sell alcohol to anyone under the age of (　　).

3) I remember being (　　) years old at the time of the Cuban Missile Crisis.

4) He was relatively poor in his mid-(　　) and wanted fame and distinction.

5) Under new European age discrimination rules, a default retirement age of (　　) will be introduced.

6) Some birds may well live for over (　　) years.

7) There is a (　　)-year age gap between Alice and John.

8) He is in prison for a total of just over (　　) years for killing a man in an unprovoked attack.

9) Sarah, who has been working for over (　　) years, is an experienced worker but gets paid less than Mary.

10) Mourners lined the route of the funeral of the (　　)-year-old R&B star.

解 答

1) Tributes are paid to the former bishop who died at the age of (76) after a long illness.
　　[長い闘病の後、76歳で亡くなった前司祭に、追悼が捧げられる]

2) He said it is an offense to sell alcohol to anyone under the age of (18).
   [18歳未満の者に、アルコールを販売するのは、違法行為であると彼は言った]

3) I remember being (7) years old at the time of the Cuban Missile Crisis.
   [キューバミサイル危機のとき、私は7歳だったことを覚えている]

4) He was relatively poor in his mid-(40s) and wanted fame and distinction.
   [彼は40代の半ばで、かなり貧しく、有名になることを望んでいた]

5) Under new European age discrimination rules, a default retirement age of (65) will be introduced.
   [新しいヨーロッパの年齢差別規則の下では、標準退職年齢は65歳と設定される]

   default retirement age　標準退職年齢
   ＊雇用者が強制退職年齢（mandatory retirement age）の必要性を立証しなくても、その年齢に達すれば強制退職できるよう国が定めた年齢です。

6) Some birds may well live for over (80) years.
   [80年以上生きられる鳥もいる]

7) There is a (41)-year age gap between Alice and John.
   [アリスとジョンには、41歳の年齢差がある]

8) He is in prison for a total of just over (20) years for killing a man in an unprovoked attack.
   [彼は正当な理由なく1人の男性を殺害し、合計20年あまりの期間、拘置されている]

9) Sarah, who has been working for over (15) years, is an experienced worker but gets paid less than Mary.
   [サラは15年以上働いていて経験を積んでいるが、メアリーよりも給料が低い]

10) Mourners lined the route of the funeral of the (22)-year-old R&B star.
    [追悼の人々が、享年22歳のR&Bスターの葬儀に参列するため、列をなした]

    R&B = rhythm and blues　リズムアンドブルース

🔘 TRACK 17

2 CDから流れてくる日本語を聴き、即座に英語に直して発話してください。（＊日本語の後ポーズがあって、その後すぐに英語が流れます）

1)
2)
3)
4)
5)

【解 答】

1) 47歳　　　　　　　forty-seven years old
2) 20代の半ばで　　　in one's mid-20s
3) 6歳のとき　　　　 at the age of 6
4) 18歳以上　　　　　18 or over、18 and older、18 years old and older
5) 10歳以下　　　　　10 or under、10 years old or younger

3 以下の日本語を英語に直して発話してください。　🔘 TRACK 18

1) 12歳未満の乗客

2) 39歳の大学講師

3) 14歳のロンドン出身の女子

4) 5ヵ月の赤ちゃん

5) 60歳より上の人々

【解 答】

1) passengers under the age of 12
2) a 39 year-old college lecturer
3) a 14-year-old girl from London
4) a 5-month-old baby
5) people over 60

3 ビジネス、金融、家計
Business、Market、Household Economy

通貨、為替　Currency、Currency Exchange

通貨

￥や＄などの通貨単位の記号は数字の前に置き、¢やpなどの補助単位は数字の後に置きます。

円　JPY = JP￥ = Japanese yen

【硬貨6種類】

1円硬貨	a one-yen coin、￥1 coin
5円硬貨	a five-yen coin、￥5 coin
10円硬貨	a ten-yen coin、￥10 coin
50円硬貨	a fifty-yen coin、￥50 coin
100円硬貨	a (one-) hundred-yen coin、￥100 coin
500円硬貨	a five-hundred-yen coin、￥500 coin

【紙幣4種類】

千円札	a thousand-yen bill / note、￥1,000 bill / note
二千円札	a two-thousand-yen bill / note、￥2,000 bill / note
五千円札	a five-thousand-yen bill / note、￥5,000 bill / note
一万円札	a ten-thousand-yen bill / note、￥10,000 bill / note

＊yenは単複同形です。

☐ Two ten-thousand-yen bills、Two ten-thousands
　［一万円札2枚］
☐ Three five-hundred-yen coins、Three five-hundreds
　［500円硬貨3枚］

米ドル　USD = US$ = US dollar

【硬貨6種類】
- 1セント硬貨　　a one-cent coin、1¢、a penny
- 5セント硬貨　　a five-cent coin、5¢、a nickel
- 10セント硬貨　　a ten-cent coin、10¢、a dime
- 25セント硬貨　　a twenty-five-cent coin、25¢、a quarter
- 50セント硬貨　　a fifty-cent coin、50¢、a half-dollar
- 1ドル硬貨　　a (one-) dollar coin、$1 coin

【紙幣7種類】
- 1ドル紙幣　　a (one-) dollar bill、$1 bill、a one
- 2ドル紙幣　　a two-dollar bill、$2 bill
- 5ドル紙幣　　a five-dollar bill、$5 bill、a five
- 10ドル紙幣　　a ten-dollar bill、$10 bill、a ten
- 20ドル紙幣　　a twenty-dollar bill、$20 bill、a twenty
- 50ドル紙幣　　a fifty-dollar bill、$50 bill、a fifty
- 100ドル紙幣　　a (one-) hundred-dollar bill、$100 bill、a hundred

□ Four nickels, two dimes, three quarters.
　　［5セント硬貨4枚、10セント硬貨2枚、25セント硬貨3枚］

□ Do you have a dollar (bill)? / Do you have a buck?
　　［1ドル（札）持っていますか］
　　　＊ buck は $1 です。$10 を ten bucks、$50 を fifty bucks のように、buck は dollar と同じくらいよく使います。

□ Five hundred-dollar bills、Five hundreds
　　［100ドル札5枚］

□ Three ten-dollar bills、Three tens
　　［10ドル紙幣3枚］

〈その他〉

□ The project cost us about five grand.
　　［そのプロジェクトは、約5,000ドルの費用がかかった］
　　　＊ grand は $1,000 です。単複同形です。

| 英国ポンド　　GBP = GP£= Great Britain Pound

【硬貨 8 種類】　　＊ pence = penny の複数形。"pee" と略して発音することもあります。

1 ペニー硬貨	a penny、1p
2 ペンス硬貨	a two-pence piece、2p
5 ペンス硬貨	a five-pence piece、5p
10 ペンス硬貨	a ten-pence piece、10p
20 ペンス硬貨	a twenty-pence piece、20p
50 ペンス硬貨	a fifty-pence piece、50p
1 ポンド硬貨	a one-pound coin、£1 coin、a quid
2 ポンド硬貨	a two-pound coin、£2 coin、two pounds

【紙幣 4 種類】

5 ポンド紙幣	a five-pound note、£5 note、a five、a fiver
10 ポンド紙幣	a ten-pound note、£10 note、a ten、a tenner
20 ポンド紙幣	a twenty-pound note、£20 note、a twenty
50 ポンド紙幣	a fifty-pound note、£50 note、a fifty

| ユーロ　　EUR = € = Euro

【硬貨 8 種類】

1 ユーロセント硬貨	a (one-) euro cent coin、1¢ coin、€0.01
2 ユーロセント硬貨	a two-euro cent coin、2¢ coin、€0.02
5 ユーロセント硬貨	a five-euro cent coin、5¢ coin、€0.05
10 ユーロセント硬貨	a ten-euro cent coin、10¢ coin、€0.10
20 ユーロセント硬貨	a twenty-euro cent coin、20¢ coin、€0.20
50 ユーロセント硬貨	a fifty-euro cent coin、50¢ coin、€0.50
1 ユーロ硬貨	a one-euro coin、€1 coin
2 ユーロ硬貨	a two-euro coin、€2 coin

【紙幣 7 種類】

5 ユーロ紙幣	a five-euro note、€5 note
10 ユーロ紙幣	a ten-euro note、€10 note
20 ユーロ紙幣	a twenty-euro note、€20 note
50 ユーロ紙幣	a fifty-euro note、€50 note
100 ユーロ紙幣	a (one-) hundred-euro note、€100 note

200 ユーロ紙幣	a two-hundred-euro note、€200 note
500 ユーロ紙幣	a five-hundred-euro note、€500 note

その他の通貨

韓国：ウォン	W = won
中国：人民元	RMB (renminbi) = Chinese yuan

為替

為替レート、換算

☐ Japanese firms begin to lose money at an exchange rate below ¥112 to the dollar.
　　［日本企業は、為替レート1ドル112円以下で、赤字を抱え始める］
☐ She changed British pounds to US dollars when the exchange rate was £1 = $2.82.
　　［彼女は、為替レート1ポンド2.82ドルのときに、ポンドをドルに換えた］
☐ One dollar cost about 121 yen, while one euro cost about 110 yen.
　　［1ドルは約121円で、1ユーロは約110円だった］
☐ When the project started, one pound was worth almost two dollars.
　　［プロジェクトが始まったとき、1ポンドはほぼ2ドルの価値があった］
☐ The dollar lost 2% against the euro.
　　［1ドルは、ユーロ換算で2％減価した］
☐ Each melon sells for ¥10,000 equivalent to about $83.
　　［メロン1個は1万円で売られており、それは約83ドルに相当する］

両替

☐ I would like to convert 100,000 yen into dollars.
　　［10万円をドルに両替したいのですが］
☐ Can you exchange 30,000 yen for Australian dollars?
　　［3万円をオーストラリア・ドルに両替してもらえませんか］
☐ Can you break this twenty into a ten, a five and five ones?
　　［この20ドル札を、10ドル札1枚、5ドル札1枚、1ドル札5枚に両替して

もらえませんか]

変動相場

- The E.U.'s monetary committee revalued the Irish currency, the punt, by three percent in 1998.
  ［1998 年、EU 通貨評議会（現在の経済金融評議会）は、アイルランド通貨プントを 3％切り上げた］
  　　punt　アイルランドの通貨単位・プント（ポンド）
- Bangladesh devalued its currency, the taka, by four percent.
  ［バングラデシュ政府は、通貨タカを 4％切り下げた］
  　　taka　バングラデシュの通貨単位・タカ
- The government lowered the exchange rate, so the pound is now worth $2.40.
  ［政府は為替レートを引き下げ、現在 1 ポンドは 2 ドル 40 セントだ］
- The dollar dropped 7% against the yen on Wednesday.
  ［水曜日に 7％の円高ドル安になった］

固定相場

- The peso was previously pegged at one-to-one with the dollar.
  ［ペソは、かつて 1 ドル 1 ペソの固定相場制だった］
  　　peso　中南米諸国の通貨単位・ペソ
- The exchange rate was fixed at FRF1 = CFAF100.
  ［1 フランスフラン 100CFA フランの固定相場制だった］
  　　FRF = French Franc　フランスの通貨単位・フラン
  　　CFAF = franc de la Communauté Financière d'Afrique
  　　　　　　　　　　　　西アフリカ諸国の通貨単位・CFA フラン

売買、取引

- Currency traders buy and sell $1.5 trillion every day.
  ［為替トレーダーは、毎日 1 兆 5 千億ドル売買する］
- The dollar was trading at 107.12 yen at 0800 GMT.
  ［グリニッジ標準時 8 時には、1 ドル 107 円 12 銭で取引されていた］

7 通貨、為替・徹底トレーニング Step 1

1 CDから流れてくる英文を聴き、カッコの部分を書き取ってください。

1) The pound fell back from Thursday's (   )-week high against the dollar, slipping (   )% to $(   ).

2) China's currency has been fixed at (   ) yuan to the U.S. dollar for (   ) years.

3) By (   ) GMT, one euro cost (   ) p while sterling stood at $(   ).

4) Instead of an exchange rate of (   ) euros to the pound, the department store showed an exchange rate of (   ) euros to the pound.

5) The dollar bought (   ) yen as of midday, down (   ) yen from last Thursday.

6) The official rate has been set at (   ) kronor to the euro.

7) The exchange rate is (   ) francs to the euro.

8) The president's remarks pushed the value of the yen down to (   ) per dollar from (   ).

9) In (   ) days the dollar dropped (   )% against the yen. And against the Deutsche Mark, the dollar was worth only (   ) DM, as against (   ) DM on Tuesday.

10) The Indonesian rupiah led the recovery on Tuesday with a (   )% rise. The Malaysian dollar has seen a (   )% rise.

> 解　答

1) The pound fell back from Thursday's (seven)-week high against the dollar, slipping (0.25)% to $(1.6075).
   ［木曜日の 7 週間ぶりの高値から 0.25%反落して、1 ポンド 1.6075 ドルとなった］

2) China's currency has been fixed at (8.28) yuan to the U.S. dollar for (10) years.
   ［中国の通貨は、ここ 10 年間 1 ドル 8.28 元に固定されてきた］

3) By (1700) GMT, one euro cost (71.3)p while sterling stood at $(1.65).
   ［グリニッジ標準時 17 時までに、1 ユーロは 71.3 ペンスになり、1 ポンドは 1 ドル 65 セントになった］
   　　　　sterling = pound sterling　英国の通貨単位・ポンド

4) Instead of an exchange rate of (1.6) euros to the pound, the department store showed an exchange rate of (0.6) euros to the pound.
   ［そのデパートでは、1 ポンド 1.6 ユーロではなく、1 ポンド 0.6 ユーロの為替レートと表示していた］

5) The dollar bought (116.86) yen as of midday, down (5.50) yen from last Thursday.
   ［正午の時点で、1 ドル 116 円 86 銭で買われ、先週の木曜日から 5 円 50 銭の下落となった］

6) The official rate has been set at (30.1260) kronor to the euro.
   ［公式レートでは、1 ユーロ 30.1260 クローナに設定されている］
   　　　krona　スウェーデンの通貨単位・クローナ　複数形は、kronor

7) The exchange rate is (6.55957) francs to the euro.
   ［為替レートは、1 ユーロ 6.55957 フランだ］
   　　　franc　フランス、スイス、ベルギーなどの通貨単位・フラン

8) The president's remarks pushed the value of the yen down to (132.80) per dollar from (132.55).
   ［大統領の発言により、1 ドル 132 円 55 銭から 132 円 80 銭まで円安が進んだ］

9) In (two) days the dollar dropped (15)% against the yen. And against the Deutsche Mark, the dollar was worth only (1.59) DM, as against (1.63) DM on Tuesday.

  [2日間で15%の円高ドル安になった。そして、対ドイツマルク相場は、火曜日は1ドル1.63マルクだったが、1ドルわずか1.59マルクの価値までの下落であった]

  DM = Deutsche Mark　ドイツの通貨単位・マルク

10) The Indonesian rupiah led the recovery on Tuesday with a (30)% rise. The Malaysian dollar has seen a (9)% rise.

  [インドネシアルピアは、火曜日には30%上昇で回復した。マレーシアドルは、9%の上昇が見られる]

  Indonesian rupiah = Rp.　インドネシアの通貨単位・ルピア
  Malaysian dollar = Ringgit = MYR
  　　　　　　　　　マレーシアの通貨単位・リンギット＝マレーシアドル

🅾 TRACK 20

2 CDから流れてくる日本語を聴き、即座に英語に直して発話してください。(＊日本語の後ポーズがあって、その後すぐに英語が流れます)

1)　　　　　　　　　　2)
3)　　　　　　　　　　4)
5)

解答

1) 25セント硬貨　　　　　a quarter
2) 50セント硬貨　　　　　a half-dollar
3) 2ペンス硬貨　　　　　a two-pence piece
4) 10ポンド紙幣　　　　　a ten-pound note、a tenner、a ten
5) 50ユーロ紙幣　　　　　a fifty-euro note

3 以下の日本語を英語に直して発話してください。　🅾 TRACK 21

1) 1ドル88円10銭へ下落した。

2) 1ドル90円以上に反発した。

3） 円は 1 ドル 104 円 52 銭まで上昇した。

4） 外国為替市場での 20 億ドルの損失

5） ディナールは 10%上昇した。

【解 答】

1) The dollar fell to 88.10 yen.
2) The dollar bounced back to above 90 yen.
3) The yen rose as high as 104.52 per dollar.
4) lost $2 billion on the foreign currency market
5) The Iraqi dinar rose by 10%.
　　　Iraqi dinar　イラクの通貨単位・ディナール

株式、債券　Stocks、Bonds

株　式

株

□ Shares were offered to the public as well as company employees at around $2.50 per share.
　　［従業員だけでなく一般にも、株が1株あたり約2.50ドルで販売された］
□ Technology stocks in Europe fell 5.5 percent overall on Wednesday.
　　［ヨーロッパのテクノロジー株は、水曜日、全体的に5.5％下落した］

銘　柄

□ Issues listed: 1,885 companies, 2,426 issues.
　　［上場銘柄：1,885社、2,426銘柄］

株式市場

□ The U.S. stock market lost 90 percent of its peak value in 3 years.
　　［アメリカ株式市場は、過去3年間でピーク時の90％価値を失った］

〈主な証券取引所と株式市場〉
□ Tokyo Stock Exchange = TSE　　　東京証券取引所
□ New York Stock Exchange = NYSE　ニューヨーク証券取引所
□ London Stock Exchange = LSE　　　ロンドン証券取引所
□ National Association of Securities Dealers Automated Quotations
　= NASDAQ　　　　　　　　　　　米国店頭株式市場、ナスダック

株価指数

□ The "All Share Price Index" shed 125 points to close at 1,188.
　　［株価指数は、125ポイント安の1,188で終えた］
　　＊"All Share Price Index" という名のついた株価指数は、複数あります。

☐ The Korea Composite Stock Price Index rose 0.60% to 613.63 points as trading began.
  ［韓国総合株価指数は、取引開始時点で 0.60%上がって 613.63 になった］
  Korea Composite Stock Price Index ＝ KOSPI　韓国総合株価指数

東証株価指数

☐ The Tokyo Stock Price Index (TOPIX), a composite of all First Section-listed issues fell 6 points to 1,263.
  ［東証一部上場全銘柄を対象とする東証株価指数（トピックス）は、6 ポイント下落して 1,263 になった］

ナスダック総合指数

☐ The Nasdaq Composite Index was up 5.63 at 2443.83.
  ［ナスダック総合指数は、5.63 ポイント高の 2443.83 だった］

平均株価

☐ The average stock price for companies making up the S&P 500 is $30.
  ［S&P 500 を構成している企業の平均株価は、30 ドルである］
    ＊ S&P 500（＝エスアンドピー 500）は、アメリカの投資会社 Standard & Poor's 社が算出している、アメリカの代表的な株価指数です。

株価変動

☐ The share price of the software giant fell 14.5%.
  ［最大手のソフトウェア会社の株価は、14.5%下落した］
☐ The stock price has dropped by nearly 70% this year.
  ［その株価は、今年 70%近く下落している］
☐ M&S stock hit its all-time high of $55 in February.
  ［2 月に M&S の株価は、過去最高の 55 ドルの値が付いた］
☐ Its share price has gone up by more than 1,300% to $338.
  ［その株価は、1,300%以上値上がりして、338 ドルになった］

- The stock opened at $76, up $23.
  [その株は、23ドル高の76ドルで寄り付いた]
- The stock closed $4.16 lower at $49.52.
  [その株は、4ドル16セント安の49ドル52セントで引けた]

日経平均株価

- The Nikkei Average was down 697.51 points, or 4.2%, to 15,836.36.
  [日経平均株価は、697.51ポイント安（4.2%）で15,836円36銭になった]

ダウ（・ジョーンズ）工業平均株価

- The Dow Jones Industrial Average soared by 131 points to 9,407.
  [ダウ工業平均株価は、131ポイント急上昇し9,407ドルになった]

株の売買、出来高

- He traded stock worth more than half a million pounds in December.
  [彼は12月に、50万ポンド以上の株の売買をした]
- Investors bought $1,000 worth of shares.
  [投資家たちは、1,000ドル分の株を購入した]
- Today's volume on the First Section of the Tokyo Stock Exchange was estimated at 3.2286 billion shares.
  [東証一部の今日の出来高は、概算で32億2,860万株だった]

経営権

- They hold a 15% stake in the Anglo-Irish Bank.
  [彼らは、アングロ-アイリッシュ銀行の経営権の15%を保有している]

時価総額

- The merger will result in a market capitalization of between DM 8 bn and DM 12 bn.
    [合併によって、時価総額は 80 〜 120 億マルクになるだろう]
    DM = Deutsche mark　ドイツの通貨単位・マルク

配　当

- The full-year dividend was increased to 3.70p from 3.06p last year.
    [1 年間の配当は、去年の 3.06 ペンスから 3.70 ペンスに上がった]

含み益、含み損

- The venture had a net unrealized gain of $450,000.
    [そのベンチャー企業は、45 万ドルの純含み益を出した]
- The company has made a paper loss of at least £36M.
    [その会社は、少なくとも 3,600 万ポンドの含み損を抱えている]

株式分割

- The company declared a 2-for-1 stock split.
    [その企業は、2 対 1 の株式分割を発表した]

その他

□ 上げ相場	bull market
□ 下げ相場	bear market
□ マーケットの調整局面	correction
□ 空売り（の）	short
□ 株主資本、普通株	equity
□ 株式公開買い付け	takeover bid、TOB

債 券

債 券

☐ The telecoms company intends to raise more than $50M through a bond issue to expand its mobile phone operations.
　[その通信会社は、携帯電話業務の拡大を図るために、5,000万ドル以上を債権の発行によって調達しようとしている]

国 債

☐ The country plans to reduce the amount of 10-year government bonds to be issued in February.
　[国は、2月に発行される10年物国債の発行額を、減らす予定である]

☐ They were arrested in London and charged with attempting a $25 billion U.S. bond fraud.
　[彼らはロンドンで逮捕され、250億ドルの米国債権詐欺未遂容疑で、告発された]

投 資

☐ The £350-million investment will upgrade the facility.
　[3億5,000万ポンドの投資で、その施設の改良をする]

☐ The finance ministry announced an increase in the tax-free allowance on profits from stock investment to 150,000 rupees from 100,000 rupees.
　[財務省は、株式投資から得た利益に対する非課税控除枠を、従来の10万ルピーから15万ルピーに増額すると発表した]
　　rupee　インド、パキスタン、スリランカの通貨単位・ルピー

8 株式、債券・徹底トレーニング Step 1

🎧 TRACK 22

1 CDから流れてくる英文を聴き、カッコの部分を書き取ってください。

1) Shares of the company fell almost $(　　) to $(　　) in early trading in New York.

2) The shares dropped (　　)% to (　　)p ― (　　)p less than the issue price (　　) weeks ago.

3) TOPIX or Tokyo Stock Price Index composite of all issues listed on the exchange's first section closed down (　　)%, at (　　).

4) The Nikkei Stock Average ended down (　　) points or (　　) percent.

5) Profits have more than tripled to £(　　) m, and its market capitalization now stands above £(　　) bn.

6) Its share price ― $(　　) a couple of months ago ― slumped to $(　　).

7) The company bought a (　　)% stake in the club in April (　　).

8) Stocks fell last week as the yield of the benchmark (　　)-year government bond surged to a (　　)-month high among fears of oversupply.

9) The Kuwait Stock Exchange closed down more than (　　)% after losing (　　)% on Monday. Its tech stock index performed better with a rise of (　　).

10) Its share price has gone from $(　　) last March to $(　　) this week.

解　答

1) Shares of the company fell almost $(15) to $(91.50) in early trading in New York.
   [その企業の株価は、ニューヨークでの取引開始後まもなく、ほぼ 15 ドル下落し、91 ドル 50 セントになった]

2) The shares dropped (13)% to (135)p — (15)p less than the issue price (eight) weeks ago.
   [株価は、13％下落して 135 ペンスになった。8 週間前の発行価格の 15 ペンス安]

3) TOPIX or Tokyo Stock Price Index composite of all issues listed on the exchange's first section closed down (0.28)%, at (1,328.9).
   [東証一部上場全銘柄を対象とする株価指数であるトピックスは、0.28％下がって 1,328.9 で取引を終えた]

4) The Nikkei Stock Average ended down (159.5) points or (1.63) percent.
   [日経平均は、159.5 ポイント、1.63％下落して取引を終えた]

5) Profits have more than tripled to £(933) m, and its market capitalization now stands above £(4) bn.
   [収益は 3 倍以上の 9 億 3,300 万ポンドで、時価総額は現在 40 億ポンド以上である]

6) Its share price — $(120) a couple of months ago — slumped to $(85).
   [その株価は、数ヵ月前は 120 ドルだったが、85 ドルに暴落した]

7) The company bought a (20)% stake in the club in April (2008).
   [その企業は、2008 年 4 月に、クラブの経営権の 20％を買い取った]

8) Stocks fell last week as the yield of the benchmark (10)-year government bond surged to a (19)-month high among fears of oversupply.
   [供給過多の不安の中、10 年物の国債代表銘柄の利回りが 19 ヵ月ぶりの高水準に急騰したため、株価は先週下落した]

9) The Kuwait Stock Exchange closed down more than (2.5)% after losing (3.5)% on Monday. Its tech stock index performed better with a rise of (6.75).
   [クウェート証券取引所は、月曜日に 3.5％下落した後、2.5％以上の下落で取引終了した。テクノロジー関連株指数は、6.75 上昇した]

10) Its share price has gone from $(450) last March to $(348) this week.
   [その株価は、3月の450ドルから今週は348ドルになっている]

TRACK 23

2 CDから流れてくる日本語を聴き、即座に英語に直して発話してください。(＊日本語の後ポーズがあって、その後すぐに英語が流れます)

1)   2)
3)   4)
5)

【解答】

1) 額面1ポンドに対し25ペンスの配当   a dividend of 25p on the pound
2) 2：1の株式分割   two-for-one stock split
3) 今日の出来高：概算19億株   Today's volume: estimated 1.9 billion
4) 30優良銘柄   30 blue chip issues
5) 5年債   five-year bonds

3 以下の日本語を英語に直して発話してください。   TRACK 24

1) その株価が15％値上がりした。

2) 11％以上、株価が下がった。

3) 株価は5ドル急騰した。

4) 彼らは、配当を5.9ペンスに上げた。

5) 30年物の国債の利回りは、6％に達する。

【解答】

1) Its share price has gone up by 15%.
2) The share price fell more than 11%.
3) The shares surged five dollars.
4) They increased the dividend to 5.9p.
5) The 30-year bond's yield hits 6%.

売上げ、利益、損益（費用）　Sales、Profit、Loss（Cost）

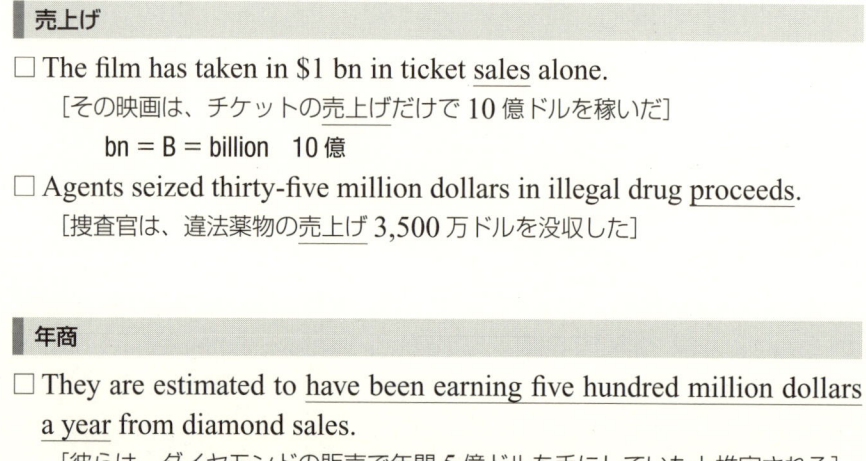

売上げ

売上げ

☐ The film has taken in $1 bn in ticket sales alone.
　　［その映画は、チケットの売上げだけで10億ドルを稼いだ］
　　　　bn = B = billion　10億
☐ Agents seized thirty-five million dollars in illegal drug proceeds.
　　［捜査官は、違法薬物の売上げ3,500万ドルを没収した］

年商

☐ They are estimated to have been earning five hundred million dollars a year from diamond sales.
　　［彼らは、ダイヤモンドの販売で年間5億ドルを手にしていたと推定される］
☐ They announced that their annual turnover is nearing the £1 m mark.
　　［彼らは年間総売上げが、100万ポンド台に迫っていると公表した］
　　　　m = M = MM = mm = million　100万
☐ The new business is expected to have annual sales of over £1 bn.
　　［新事業は、年商10億ポンド以上と期待されている］

利　益

歳入、税収、収入

☐ Uganda announced a big increase in its goverment revenue from two to ten million U.S. dollars.
　　［ウガンダ政府は、歳入が200万米ドルから1,000万米ドルへと大きく増加したと発表した］
☐ In the U.K., the tobacco industry generated over £10 bn in tax revenue in 1998.
　　［イギリスでは、1998年にたばこ産業が、100億ポンド以上の税収を生み出した］

☐ The corporation managed to surpass one billion dollars in total revenue in just 22 years.
　［その企業はわずか22年間で、総収入10億ドルを達成した］

利益

☐ They confirmed a year-end operating profit of £1.4 M.
　［彼らは、140万ポンドの年度末営業利益を発表した］
☐ Los Angeles made a record profit of $220 M when it hosted the 1984 Olympics.
　［ロサンゼルスは、1984年に主催したオリンピックで、2億2,000万ドルという記録的な利益を上げた］
☐ The bank is on track to record an annual profit of more than £5.3 bn.
　［その銀行は、年間利益53億ポンド以上を記録する見込みである］

純益

☐ The software company posted a net profit of $42 MM last year.
　［そのソフトウェア会社は、昨年、4,200万ドルの純益を計上した］
☐ Northern Irish farmers made a net gain of more than £6 MM.
　［北アイルランドの農夫たちは、600万ポンド以上の純益を得た］

黒字

☐ The surplus was 3.8 billion dollars in October.
　［黒字額は、10月は38億ドルだった］

損益（費用）

歳出、歳費

☐ The government allocated 5% of its budget spending for the poor.
　［政府は、歳出の5%を貧困層へ配分した］

☐ The new county council will have an annual expenditure of nearly £750 M.
　［新しい州議会は、約 7 億 5,000 万ポンドの年間歳費を計上する］

損　失

☐ In December, the global air transport industry announced they would make a combined loss of $2.5 bn.
　［12 月には、世界の航空輸送業界は 25 億ドルの損失を出すだろうと発表した］

赤　字

☐ The U.S. trade balance worsened to a record deficit of $24.62 billion in June.
　［米国の貿易収支は悪化し、6 月には記録的な 246 億 2,000 万ドルの赤字となった］

9 売上げ、利益、損益（費用）・徹底トレーニング Step 1

1 CD から流れてくる英文を聴き、カッコの部分を書き取ってください。

1) The club is understood to have doubled its turnover from last year to almost £(   ) M.

2) The society estimates that annual sales will reach around ¥(   ) million — roughly the same figure as in (   ).

3) The chief executive announced an increase in turnover to £(   ) MM but saw a dip in profits in the club's interim results.

4) Total revenue was $(   ) bn, up (   )% compared with the same quarter in the previous year.

5) One of the creditors got (   ) U.S. dollars from the sale of the equipment.

6) The company expects a (   )-billion-dollar operating loss by the end of the fiscal year.

7) In (   ), the wine company from California generated $(   ) billion worth of sales.

8) Iraq was allowed to exchange (   ) billion dollars of oil sales for food and medical supplies every (   ) months.

9) The first quarter revenues are likely to be at least $(   ) M {£(   ) M} lower.

10) The world's biggest bank by market value says that its net profit for (   ) rose by (   ), setting a record for the bank.

解 答

1) The club is understood to have doubled its turnover from last year to almost £(6.8) M.
   [そのクラブは、総売上げが昨年の2倍、約680万ポンドになったと推定されている]

2) The society estimates that annual sales will reach around ¥(2.25) million — roughly the same figure as in (2007).
   [協会は、年間売上げを約225万円と見込んでいるが、これは2007年の実績とほぼ同じである]

3) The chief executive announced an increase in turnover to £(46) MM but saw a dip in profits in the club's interim results.
   [その最高責任者は、総売上げ高が4,600万ポンドに増加したことを発表したが、クラブの中間決算における収益の落ち込みを予見した]

4) Total revenue was $(5.7) bn, up (18)% compared with the same quarter in the previous year.
   [歳入合計は57億ドル、前年同四半期と比較して18%の増加であった]

5) One of the creditors got (20,000) U.S. dollars from the sale of the equipment.
   [債権者の1人は、その設備の売却で2万米ドルを回収できた]

6) The company expects a (4.9)-billion-dollar operating loss by the end of the fiscal year.
   [その会社は、会計年度末までに49億ドルの営業損失を見込んでいる]

7) In (2008), the wine company from California generated $(2.7) billion worth of sales.
   [2008年には、そのカリフォルニアのワイン会社は27億ドル相当の売上げを達成した]

8) Iraq was allowed to exchange (five) billion dollars of oil sales for food and medical supplies every (six) months.
   [イラクは6ヵ月ごとに、石油売上げ50億ドルと食料・医薬品の交換を認められていた]

9) The first quarter revenues are likely to be at least $(600) M {£(434) M} lower.
   [第1四半期の総収入は、少なくとも6億ドル（4億3,400万ポンド）は減少の可能性がある]

10) The world's biggest bank by market value says that its net profit for (2008) rose by (a third), setting a record for the bank.
　　［時価総額で世界最大のその銀行は、2008年度純益が3分の1増加し、同行の純益記録を更新したと述べている］
　　　＊時価総額（market capitalization）は、market value ともいいます。

TRACK 26

2 CDから流れてくる日本語を聴き、即座に英語に直して発話してください。（＊日本語の後ポーズがあって、その後すぐに英語が流れます）

1)　　　　　　　　　　2)
3)　　　　　　　　　　4)
5)

【解答】

1) 純益8万ポンド　　　　　　　net profits of £80,000
2) 売上げ合計24億ポンド　　　　sales totaled £2.4 bn
3) 数十億ドルの黒字　　　　　　a couple of billion dollars of surplus
4) 1億円の営業損失　　　　　　a 100-million-yen operating loss
5) 3倍の利益　　　　　　　　　triple profit

3 以下の日本語を英語に直して発話してください。　　TRACK 27

1) 貿易黒字は、9,150億円に達した。

2) 純益は、24.5％下がった。

3) その会社の年商は10％伸びた。

4) その会社は、600万ドルの損失をこうむった。

5) 5億ドル超に相当する売上げ

【解答】

1) The trade surplus hit ¥915 bn.

2) Net profit was down 24.5%.
3) The company's annual sales rose 10%.
4) The company suffered a loss of $6 M.
5) over half a billion dollars' worth of sales

料金、価格　Fees / Charges / Rates / Fares、Prices

料　金

授業料、入場料など　fee

- Every year she sent me US$1,000 for school fees.
  [毎年、彼女は私に 1,000 米ドルを授業料として送ってきた]
- Entrance fees will be either $6.35 or $3.54.
  [入場料は、6 ドル 35 セントか、3 ドル 54 セントのどちらかになる]
- The cancellation fee is between $100 and $150.
  [キャンセル料は、100 ドルから 150 ドルである]

料金、使用料など　charge

- The bill is calculated at the checkout and a £5 delivery charge will be added.
  [請求額はチェックアウトの際に計算され、5 ポンドの配達料金が加算される]
- The extra room charge is 2,900 yen.
  [部屋代の延長料金は、2,900 円だ]

料金、値段など　rate

- Hotel rates have crashed to less than $90 a night.
  [ホテル料金は、1 泊 90 ドル以下にまで下がっている]
- The electric utility rate hikes a maximum of 20% a year.
  [電気料金は、年に最高で 20% 上がる]

運賃、料金など　fare

- The fare is $50 one-way, $96 roundtrip.
  [運賃は、片道 50 ドル、往復 96 ドルだ]
- Last year the airfare cost about ¥25,000.
  [去年、飛行機代は約 25,000 円だった]

その他

- ☐ 賃借料、使用料、家賃　　rent
- ☐ レンタル料金　　rental fee
- ☐ 賃貸借契約料金、リース料金　　lease fee
- ☐ 罰金　　fine
- ☐ 手数料　　commission
- ☐ 授業料　　tuition
- ☐ 観覧料、入学金、入場料　　admission fee
- ☐ 通話料金　　calling / call rate
- ☐ 使用料、印税　　royalties

価　格

価格、値段

☐ The oil price fell sharply to $92.38 a barrel.
　　［原油価格は急激に落ち込み、1 バレル 92 ドル 38 セントとなった］

☐ Diamonds cost $150,000 per carat.
　　［ダイヤモンドの値段は、1 カラットあたり 15 万ドルした］

その他

- ☐ 定価　　catalog / fixed price
- ☐ 希望価格　　asking price
- ☐ 末端価格　　retail price（小売価格）、street value（麻薬など）
- ☐ 卸売価格　　wholesale price
- ☐ 税込み価格　　price includes / with tax、tax-inclusive price
- ☐ 税抜き価格　　price before / without tax、tax-exclusive price
- ☐ 単価　　price per unit
- ☐ 物価　　price of commodity
- ☐ 時価　　current price

10 料金、価格・徹底 トレーニング Step 1

TRACK 28

1 CDから流れてくる英文を聴き、カッコの部分を書き取ってください。

1) The rate for a standard room at one hotel has exploded from US$ (　　　) to US$(　　　).

2) The company was paying $(　　　) a gallon for diesel fuel (　　　) months ago. Recently, it hit $(　　　) a gallon.

3) The fine for encroaching on a crosswalk would increase from $(　　　) to $(　　　) under a pedestrian safety proposal.

4) The contract price fell $(　　　) overnight to settle at $(　　　).

5) Commercial office space: Full service office space. Attractive, professional space starting at $(　　　) / mo. (　　　) convenient locations.

6) Gold was fixed at (　　　) dollars an ounce, down more than (　　　) dollars from Tuesday.

7) Open to members Tuesday through Friday ($(　　　) per year) and to the public on Saturdays ($(　　　) per child).

8) She and her (　　　) friends paid a taxi $(　　　) each for the roundtrip from Southampton.

9) Telephone and internet purchases will be subject to a booking fee of up to £(　　　) per ticket and a £(　　　) delivery charge per transaction.

10) Delicious selection of fresh tuna, along with (　　　) other courses and an amuse-bouche, for just €(　　　) about $(　　　) at $(　　　) to the euro.

解 答

1) The rate for a standard room at one hotel has exploded from US$ (140) to US$ (300).
   [あるホテルのスタンダードルームの料金が、140米ドルから300米ドルに急に上がった]

2) The company was paying $(2.85) a gallon for diesel fuel (18) months ago. Recently, it hit $(5.05) a gallon.
   [その会社のディーゼル燃料の支払いは、18ヵ月前は1ガロンあたり2ドル85セントだった。それが最近では、1ガロンあたり5ドル5セントにまで上昇した]

3) The fine for encroaching on a crosswalk would increase from $(50) to $(500) under a pedestrian safety proposal.
   [歩行者安全に関する提案を受けて、横断歩道侵入の罰金が50ドルから500ドルに上がる見込みだ]

4) The contract price fell $(1.81) overnight to settle at $(86.62).
   [協定価格は一晩で1ドル81セント下がって、86ドル62セントになった]

5) Commercial office space: Full service office space. Attractive, professional space starting at $(495) / mo. (Three) convenient locations.
   [商業用事務所：フルサービスで魅力のプロ仕様、月額495ドルより。好立地の物件3件あり]

6) Gold was fixed at (269.50) dollars an ounce, down more than (two) dollars from Tuesday.
   [金は、1オンスあたり296ドル50セントで値決めされた。火曜日から、2ドル以上の下落である]

7) Open to members Tuesday through Friday ($(65) per year) and to the public on Saturdays ($(5) per child).
   [会員は、火曜日から金曜日まで利用可（年会費65ドル）、一般利用は土曜日のみ（子ども1人あたり5ドル）]

8) She and her (13) friends paid a taxi $(20) each for the roundtrip from Southampton.
   [彼女と13人の友人は、サザンプトンからの往復に1人20ドルのタクシー代を支払った]

9) Telephone and internet purchases will be subject to a booking fee of up to £(3) per ticket and a £(4.85) delivery charge per transaction.
　　［電話とインターネットでの購入は、チケット1枚につき予約料最大3ポンドまで、そして1回の取引につき4.85ポンドの送料が加算される］

10) Delicious selection of fresh tuna, along with (two) other courses and an amuse-bouche, for just €(18) about $(29) at $(1.59) to the euro.
　　［アミューズブッシュと2種類の料理に、とてもおいしい新鮮なマグロ料理がついて、値段はわずか18ユーロ（1ユーロ1.59ドル換算で約29ドル）］
　　　　amuse　アミューズ＝楽しみ、bouche　ブッシュ＝口（くち）
　　　＊フランス料理で、前菜の前にいただく一口サイズの料理のことです。

TRACK 29

2　CDから流れてくる日本語を聴き、即座に英語に直して発話してください。（＊日本語の後ポーズがあって、その後すぐに英語が流れます）

1)　　　　　　　　　　　　2)
3)　　　　　　　　　　　　4)
5)

解答

1)　銅製調理器具、449ドル95セント　　　　copper cookware, $449.95
2)　ケントにある彼らの120万ポンドの家　　their £1.2 M home in Kent
3)　4月分電気代は32ドル65セントだった。
　　　　　　　　　　　　　　　　　　　　The power bill in April was $32.65.
4)　2個のお買い上げで1個無料。　　　　　Buy two, get one free.
5)　要事前登録。料金55ドル　　　　　　　Registration required. $55

3　以下の日本語を英語に直して発話してください。　TRACK 30

1)　3種類すべてのサンプルを、30ドルでお試しください。

2)　私は、ひと月60ドルを会費に使う。

3)　いくつかの商品は、1パック50セントを切る。

4) その家は、280万ドルで売り出し中である。

5) 通常価格から、20%の割引を受けられる。

解 答

1) Have a sampling of all three for $30.
2) I spend 60 bucks a month on a membership.
3) Some cost less than 50 cents a pack.
4) The house is being sold for $2.8 million.
5) You can get 20% off the usual price.

収入、支出、税金　Income、Expenses、Taxes

収　入

年収、年俸

- The maximum annual income is $100,000.
  ［最高年収は、10万ドルだ］
- The average yearly salary was £60,000.
  ［平均年収は、6万ポンドだった］
- Baseball players are paid an annual salary of ¥200 million.
  ［野球選手は、年俸2億円を支払われている］

月　収

- Average monthly earnings per full-time worker were ¥411,477.
  ［常勤労働者の平均月収は、41万1,477円だった］
- He said the minimum wage should be $3,250 / month.
  ［最低月収は3,250ドルにすべきと、彼は言った］

週給、日給、時給

- The maximum weekly salary is £350.
  ［週給の最高額は、350ポンドだ］
- The company agreed to raise basic daily pay by $70 to about $180.
  ［会社は、基本日給を70ドル上げて約180ドルにすることに同意した］
- Their starting wage is $10 an hour.
  ［彼らの時給は、10ドルから始まる］
- The average hourly wage for part-timers was ¥973.
  ［パートタイマーの平均時給は、973円だった］

税込み収入、税引き前収入、税引き後収入、手取り収入

- They will have their pre-tax income reduced by 10%.
  ［彼らの税込み収入は、10%下がる］

- ☐ A family of four living in a major city with a before-tax income of less than $37,791 is considered below the poverty line.
  ［税引き前収入 37,791 ドル以下の、大都市に住む 4 人家族は、貧困ラインを下回ると考えられている］
- ☐ His total income after taxes is more than 6.7 million yen.
  ［彼の税引き後の総収入は、670 万円以上である］
- ☐ The average after-tax annual income for a family of two or more people was $59,900.
  ［2 人以上の世帯の平均手取り年収は、59,900 ドルだった］
- ☐ This person's monthly take-home salary is £1,500.
  ［この人物の月収は、手取りで 1,500 ポンドである］

手当、小遣い

- ☐ He will collect $100,000 a year plus other benefits.
  ［彼は、1 年に 10 万ドルとその他の手当を受取る予定だ］
- ☐ The birth allowance was eight hundred dollars for every child born in the town.
  ［その町で生まれたすべての子どもに対して、出産手当は 800 ドルだった］
- ☐ A regular allowance of $5 per month was given to the younger sisters.
  ［月に 5 ドルの小遣いが、妹たちに与えられた］

ボーナス

- ☐ A ¥25,000 bonus will be paid to the staff who turns up for work during a heavy snow.
  ［大雪の際出勤する社員には、25,000 円のボーナスが支給される］

昇給、減給

- ☐ The National Union of Teachers is asking for a 10% pay raise.
  ［全国教師組合は、10％の昇給を要求している］
- ☐ We have to take a pay cut of 10-15%.
  ［われわれは、10 〜 15％の減給を受け入れなければならない］

その他

- ☐ 課税所得　　taxable income
- ☐ 奨励金　　　incentive
- ☐ 諸手当　　　fringe benefit
- ☐ 特別手当　　special allowance、special benefit

支 出

経 費

☐ Expenses : 3,000 yen (transportation fee and travel insurance).
　［経費：3,000 円（運送料および旅行保険）］

生活費

☐ The family set aside 6,000 dollars for living expenses.
　［その家族は、生活費として 6,000 ドル残しておいた］

☐ The average cost of living for a Japanese was about 100,000 yen a month.
　［日本人の 1 ヵ月の平均生活費は、約 10 万円だった］

住居費

☐ Housing expenses should not account for more than 25-30% of a person's income.
　［住居費は、個人の収入の 25 〜 30%以上にならないようにするべきだ］

食 費

☐ She was allowed 45 dollars a day in food expenses.
　［彼女は、食費として 1 日 45 ドル使うことが許されていた］

光熱費

- Heat and lighting expenses were 5,000 yen per night in summer and 12,000 yen per night in winter.
  ［光熱費は、夏期は一晩につき 5,000 円、冬期は 12,000 円だった］

その他

- 交通費　transportation expenses
- 日当　　per diem
- 医療費　medical expenses

税　金

消費税

- In Japan, a consumption tax is levied on all retail items — it is currently 5% of the product's price.
  ［日本では、消費税はすべての小売商品に課せられ、現在、商品価格の 5% である］

所得税

- He was arrested for allegedly evading $759,500 in income tax.
  ［彼は、所得税 759,500 ドルを脱税したとして逮捕された］

住民税

- The City Council approved a residential tax increase of 5.75%.
  ［市議会は、住民税の 5.75%の値上げを可決した］

税金還付

- They lost their appeal in a dispute over a tax refund of more than $300,000.
  ［彼らの30万ドル以上の税金還付に関する紛争の上告は、棄却された］

その他

- （所得税の）納税申告書　　　（income）tax return
- 控除　　　　　　　　　　　　deduction
- 売上げ税（米）　　　　　　　sales tax
- 付加価値税（英、欧州など）　VAT（= value added tax）

＊ sales tax と VAT は、日本の consumption tax にあたります。

11 収入、支出、税金・徹底トレーニング Step 1

1 CDから流れてくる英文を聴き、カッコの部分を書き取ってください。

1) The workers rejected an offer of a (　　)% wage hike and a (　　)-Canadian-dollar bonus.

2) Most of the garment workers worked well over the legal (　　) hours per week for between $(　　) and $(　　) per month.

3) Senior tax panel officials approved a proposal for a (　　)% cut in personal income tax and a (　　)% cut in residential tax.

4) The Fire Brigades' Union is calling for a (　　)% pay raise to give fully qualified firefighters a minimum annual wage of £(　　).

5) The space heating energy requirements typically amount to less than (　　)kWh per heating season, or less than C$(　　).

6) If your purchase today amounts to ¥(　　) more, you will be exempt from paying the (　　)% consumption tax.

7) They are able to get tax refunds ranging between £(　　) and £(　　) a year.

8) Chinese women have asked for their monthly after-tax pay to double, from $(　　) to $(　　).

9) Day center workers have to pay £(　　) for their meals and £(　　) towards travel expenses.

10) They agreed to a (　　)-year, $(　　)-million contract that comes with a $(　　)-million signing bonus.

解 答

1) The workers rejected an offer of a (3.25)% wage hike and a (1,000)-Canadian-dollar bonus.
　　［従業員は、（企業からの）3.25%の昇給と 1,000 カナダドルのボーナスの申し出を拒否した］

2) Most of the garment workers worked well over the legal (48) hours per week for between $(30) and $(40) per month.
　　［ほとんどの衣料産業労働者は、月収 30〜40 ドルで、法定労働時間である週 48 時間を、ゆうに超えて働いていた］

3) Senior tax panel officials approved a proposal for a (20)% cut in personal income tax and a (15)% cut in residential tax.
　　［税制調査会の上級委員は、個人所得税 20%カット、住民税 15%カットの提案を承諾した］

4) The Fire Brigades' Union is calling for a (40)% pay raise to give fully qualified firefighters a minimum annual wage of £(30,000).
　　［消防士組合は、条件を十分に満たしている消防士への 40%の賃上げによる、最低年収 3 万ポンドの確保を要求している］

5) The space heating energy requirements typically amount to less than (10,000)kWh per heating season, or less than C$(1,000).
　　［この場所の暖房エネルギーは、通常 1 暖房期につき 1 万キロワットアワー以下、つまり 1,000 カナダドル以下となっている］

6) If your purchase today amounts to ¥(10,001) more, you will be exempt from paying the (5)% consumption tax.
　　［本日、お客様の購入代金が 1 万 1 円以上だった場合、5%の消費税のお支払いが免除されます］

7) They are able to get tax refunds ranging between £(600) and £(3,000) a year.
　　［彼らは、年間 600〜3,000 ポンドの税金還付を受けることができる］

8) Chinese women have asked for their monthly after-tax pay to double, from $(350) to $(700).
　　［中国人女性が、月給の手取り額を現在の 350 ドルから 2 倍の 700 ドルに増やすよう要求している］

9) Day center workers have to pay £(2.30) for their meals and £(1.50) towards travel expenses.
　　［デイセンターの職員は、彼らの食費に 2 ポンド 30 ペンス、交通費に 1 ポンド 50 ペンスを支払わなければならない］

10) They agreed to a (seven)-year, $(46)-million contract that comes with a $(11)-million signing bonus.
　　［彼らは、1,100 万ドルの契約ボーナスを含む、7 年間 4,600 万ドルの契約に同意した］
　　＊契約ボーナス＝契約締結時に支払われるボーナス

🅾 TRACK 32

2 CD から流れてくる日本語を聴き、即座に英語に直して発話してください。（＊日本語の後ポーズがあって、その後すぐに英語が流れます）

1)
2)
3)
4)
5)

解 答

1) 0.5%の昇給　　　　　　　a 0.5% pay rise
2) 10%の賃金カット　　　　a 10-percent cut in wages
3) 400 ドルの手当　　　　　400 dollars in benefits
4) 2,000 ポンドの旅費　　　£2,000 in travel expenses
5) 一律 5%の消費税　　　　the flat rate of 5% consumption tax

3 以下の日本語を英語に直して発話してください。　🅾 TRACK 33

1) 毎月の必要経費の平均は、201,238 円だった。

2) 彼女は、300 ドルのボーナスの支払いを拒否した。

3) 時給は、67 ドルに減らされた。

4) 彼らの基本生活費は、38,000 元だった。

5) 私たちは、1日350ドルの手当受給資格がある。

解 答

1) Average monthly expenses were 201,238 yen.
2) She has refused to pay the 300-dollar bonus.
3) The hourly wage was cut to 67 dollars.
4) Their basic living expenses were 38,000 yuan.
5) We are entitled to an allowance of 350 dollars per day.

ローン、クレジット、金利　Loans、Credit、Interest

ローン

ローン、融資

- Our student loan is nearly £5,000 per year.
  [われわれの学資ローンは、年間約 5,000 ポンドである]
- Crisis-hit Indonesia got a 20-billion-yen ODA loan.
  [危機的状況のインドネシアは、200 億円の政府開発援助融資を受けた]

借款

- The remaining $3.5 bn will take the form of yen loans.
  [残りの 35 億ドルについては、円借款のかたちをとる]

不良債権

- Japan's banks are burdened by at least 87.5 trillion yen in bad loans.
  [邦銀は、少なくとも 87.5 兆円の不良債権を負っている]

一括払い、分割払い

- They offered a single payment of just under one hundred and five million dollars.
  [彼らは、1 億 500 万ドル弱の支払いに、一括払いを申し出た]
- You can choose either a 6- or 12-month-installment payment plan.
  [6 ヵ月か 12 ヵ月の分割払いプランを選ぶことができる]
- Generally, you can have up to 60 months to pay.
  [一般的に、60 ヵ月までの分割払いが可能である]

頭金

- They were secured with a down payment of £250.
  [彼らは、250 ポンドの頭金を確保した]

その他

- 担保、貸付金、住宅ローン　　mortgage
- 無担保貸付金　　unsecured loan
- 未払債務、貸付残高　　outstanding loan
- サブプライム・ローン　　subprime mortgage / loan

クレジット

貸付け、融資

- The IMF approved $4.9 bn in credit for Brazil.
  ［国際通貨基金は、ブラジルに対する49億ドルの貸付けを承認した］
- The $100-million credit facility would be used only for humanitarian assistance.
  ［1億ドルの貸付金は、人道的援助にのみ利用される］
- He had talks with the Prime Minister on issuing a ten-million-dollar credit line.
  ［1,000万ドルの融資限度額を与える件で、彼は首相と会談をおこなった］

クレジットカード

- He runs up a million dollars a year on his credit card.
  ［彼のクレジットカードの年間利用限度額は、100万ドルに達する］

その他

- 信用格付　　credit rating
- 信用取引　　credit account

3 ビジネス、金融、家計

金 利

金利、利率

☐ The Bank has set a record-breaking interest rate low of 0.5%.
　［銀行は金利引下げをおこない、史上最低の金利 0.5%とした］

公定歩合

☐ The central bank lowered its discount rate by 0.5%.
　［中央銀行は、公定歩合を 0.5%引き下げた］

単利、複利

☐ Simple Interest : interest = principal × rate × time. If $100 was borrowed for 2 years at a 10% interest rate, the interest would be $100 × 0.1 × 2 = $20.
　［単利：利子＝元本×利率×期間。10%の利率で 100 ドルを 2 年間借りる場合、利子は、100 ドル× 0.1 × 2 で 20 ドルになる］

☐ £400 borrowed for 3 years at a 5% compounded interest rate.
　［400 ポンドを、3 年間、5%の複利で借りる］

TRACK 34

12　ローン、クレジット、金利・徹底トレーニング Step 1

1　CD から流れてくる英文を聴き、カッコの部分を書き取ってください。

1) The Reserve Bank of India's increase in its benchmark interest rate to (　　)% is the second in less than (　　) weeks.

2) The airline company was losing $(　　) m a day earlier this year, and so will get the bulk — or $(　　) m — of the loans.

3) The central bank governor lowered the country's discount rate by (　　) percentage points to (　　).

4) You can get loans of £(　　)-(　　) instantly.

5) The national electricity company has been given a (　　)-million-dollar loan to launch a (　　)-year program to improve power lines.

解答

1) The Reserve Bank of India's increase in its benchmark interest rate to (8.5)% is the second in less than (two) weeks.
　　［インド準備銀行による、指標金利の 8.5%への引き上げは、2 週間足らずで 2 度目となる］

2) The airline company was losing $(7) m a day earlier this year, and so will get the bulk — or $(70) m — of the loans.
　　［その航空会社は、今年の初めには、1 日あたり 700 万ドルを失っていたので、融資額の大半となる 7,000 万ドルを借り入れる］

3) The central bank governor lowered the country's discount rate by (0.5) percentage points to (3.5).
　　［中央銀行総裁は、公定歩合を 0.5%引き下げ、3.5%にした］

4) You can get loans of £(80)-(750) instantly.
　　［80 〜 750 ポンドまでの借入はすぐにできる］

5) The national electricity company has been given a (forty-five)-million-dollar loan to launch a (five)-year program to improve power lines.
   [国営電力会社は、送電線改良の5ヵ年計画に着手するため、4,500万ドルの融資を受けた]

🔘 TRACK 35

2 CDから流れてくる日本語を聴き、即座に英語に直して発話してください。(＊日本語の後ポーズがあって、その後すぐに英語が流れます)

1)　　　　　　　　　　2)
3)

解答

1) 無利息で分割払い　　　　　　no-interest loan on an installment plan
2) 280万ドルの頭金　　　　　　a $2.8-million down payment
3) 90ポンドから800ポンドのローン　　loans of between £90-800

3 以下の日本語を英語に直して発話してください。　🔘 TRACK 36

1) 18%から17%への金利引下げ

2) 私たちは、彼のために500万ユーロのローンを組んだ。

3) 20万円からの融資を提供

解答

1) cut its interest rate from 18% to 17%
2) We took out the 5-million-euro loan for him.
3) offer lines of credit starting at 200,000 yen

資産、貯蓄、負債　Assets、Savings、Debts

資 産

資産／財産、〜の価値がある

- The property is worth a lot of money, about $15 M.
  ［資産は、約 1,500 万ドルと高額だ］
- His total assets have a net worth of ¥340 m.
  ［彼の財産の合計は、正味 3 億 4,000 万円だ］
- The council will provide land valued at £1.2 m for the project.
  ［評議会は、そのプロジェクトのために 120 万ポンドの価値がある土地を提供する］
- She owns a condominium worth ¥50 MM.
  ［彼女は、5,000 万円の価値があるマンションを所有している］
  * MM = M = m = mm = million

貯 蓄

預貯金

- She saved thousands of dollars for her studies.
  ［彼女は学業のために、数千ドル貯金していた］
- I have a 10 million yen deposite in a bank.
  ［私は、銀行に 1,000 万円預金している］
- The bank facilitated nearly $13 m in cash deposits.
  ［銀行は、ほぼ 1,300 万ドルを現金預金にした］

その他

- 普通預金　　savings / ordinary account
- 定期預金　　fixed deposit、certificates of deposit
- 当座預金　　checking account / deposit
- 外貨預金　　foreign currency deposit / saving
- 郵便貯金　　postal savings deposit

| ☐ 預金残高　　bank balance
| ☐ 小切手　　　check（米）、cheque（英）
| ☐ 資金洗浄　　money laundering

負債

負債、借金

☐ Debt is expected to increase to 68% of the U.K.'s GDP next year.
　　［負債は翌年、イギリスの国内総生産の68％まで増加するだろう］
☐ She is $40,000 in debt.
　　［彼女には、4万ドルの借金がある］
☐ The money has been borrowed at 4.5% from N Trusts.
　　［資金は、Nトラストから利息4.5％で借りている］
☐ The institution owes £7.5 MM.
　　［その機関は、750万ポンドの借り入れがある］
　　　＊「ローン、融資」に関してはp.80を参照してください。

借用証書

☐ He left an IOU for £7 m in the bank's safe.
　　［彼は銀行の金庫に、700万ポンドの借用証書を残していた］
　　　IOU＝借用証書　「I owe you」の音から。

その他

☐ （借金などを）完済する	pay off、clear up / off
☐ （口座などを）凍結する	freeze
☐ （借金を）払い終わる、抹消する	write off
☐ （債務証書の）保証人	bondsperson
☐ 借り主、債務者	debtor
☐ 貸し主、債権者	creditor
☐ 自己破産	personal bankruptcy

13 資産、貯蓄、負債・徹底トレーニング Step 1

TRACK 37

1 CDから流れてくる英文を聴き、カッコの部分を書き取ってください。

1) The changeover to cheaper metals brought annual savings to the US Treasury of around $(　　) m {£(　　) m}.

2) A letter was sent demanding that (　　) U.S. dollars be put into a bank account.

3) I was expected to produce $(　　) a year and remit it to a bank in China.

4) The party owned businesses worth (　　) bn Taiwan dollars, with property firms accounting for (　　) bn Taiwan dollars.

5) The university had total assets worth (　　) billion yen at the end of the last fiscal year, including (　　) billion yen in cash and deposits.

解 答

1) The changeover to cheaper metals brought annual savings to the US Treasury of around $(25) m {£(14) m}.
　　[より安い金属への転換は、米財務省証券の年間貯蓄金、約 2,500 万ドル（1,400 万ポンド）を生んだ]

2) A letter was sent demanding that (180,000) U.S. dollars be put into a bank account.
　　[銀行口座へ、18 万米ドル入金するよう要求する手紙が送付された]

3) I was expected to produce $(100,000) a year and remit it to a bank in China.
　　[私は 1 年で 10 万ドルを稼いで、中国の銀行へ送金することになっていた]

4) The party owned businesses worth (40.5) bn Taiwan dollars, with property firms accounting for (8) bn Taiwan dollars.
　　[そのグループは、80 億台湾ドルを計上する不動産会社を含む、405 億台湾ドルの価値のある企業を所有していた]

5) The university had total assets worth (94) billion yen at the end of the last fiscal year, including (12.7) billion yen in cash and deposits.
　　［この大学は、前の会計年度末では940億円の総資産があり、それには127億円の現金と預金が含まれていた］

🅒 TRACK 38

2 CDから流れてくる日本語を聴き、即座に英語に直して発話してください。(＊日本語の後ポーズがあって、その後すぐに英語が流れます)

1)　　　　　　　　　　　2)
3)

解答

1)　900ポンドの現金預金　　　　a £900 cash deposit
2)　銀行にある300万ドル　　　　three million dollars at a bank
3)　未払いの借金85ドル　　　　an outstanding debt of 85 dollars

3　以下の日本語を英語に直して発話してください。　🅒 TRACK 39

1)　ジュネーブの銀行で、800万ドルが凍結された。

2)　会社は、彼女に50ドルの小切手を送った。

3)　彼の老後の蓄えは、7,000米ドルだ。

解答

1) The amount of $8 million was frozen in a Geneva bank.
2) The company sent her a check for fifty dollars.
3) His life savings are US$7,000.

保険、年金　Insurance、Pensions

保　険

健康保険

- Health insurance premiums have been rising at 20-25% annually.
  ［健康保険料は、毎年 20〜25％上がっている］
- You have to pay 30% of your medical fees with the National Health Insurance plan.
  ［国民健康保険制度では、医療費の自己負担率は 3 割だ］

生命保険

- There were life insurance policies totaling about £400,000.
  ［合計約 40 万ポンドの、生命保険証券があった］
- I have a 10-million-yen life insurance policy.
  ［私は、1,000 万円の生命保険に入っている］

傷害、損害保険

- The actress has her smile insured for $10 million.
  ［その女優は、自分の笑顔に 1,000 万ドルの保険を掛けている］
- This automobile insurance policy covers accidental injury up to ¥5 M.
  ［この自動車保険は、事故傷害を 500 万円まで補償する］

その他の保険、保険関連用語

- 雇用保険　　　　unemployment insurance
- 介護保険　　　　long-term care insurance
- 火災保険　　　　fire insurance
- 地震保険　　　　earthquake insurance
- 災害保険　　　　casualty insurance
- 損害保険　　　　fire-and-casualty insurance、damage insurance
- 海外旅行保険　　overseas travel insurance

☐	損害請求	damage claim
☐	満期	expiration、expiration date、maturity date
☐	受取人	beneficiary
☐	被保険者	insured / assured person
☐	保険契約者	policy holder
☐	保険の未加入者	the uninsured

年金

年金

☐ The state pension is universal, for men over 65 and women over 60.
　　[国民年金は、男性65歳以上、女性60歳以上の全国民を対象とする]
☐ Annuity rates have fallen recently nearly 9%.
　　[年金率は、最近約9%下がった]

年金関連用語

☐	国民年金	state pension、government pension plan、state-run pension plan、National Pension Plan
☐	厚生年金	employee pension、employees' pension plan
☐	遺族年金	bereaved family pension
☐	年金加入者	pensioner、plan holder
☐	年金受給者	pensioner、annuitant、recipient of a pension
☐	年金受給資格	qualified conditions、qualifying conditions
☐	年金受給資格年齢	pension eligibility age

14 保険、年金・徹底トレーニング Step 1

1 CDから流れてくる英文を聴き、カッコの部分を書き取ってください。

1) Manchester drivers pay average annual insurance premiums of £(　　) compared with a national average of £(　　).

2) They already paid $(　　) M of the $(　　) M total insurance premiums so far.

3) An agreement has been reached in a lawsuit involving his $(　　) MM {£(　　) MM} life insurance policy.

4) They want the government to increase the basic state pension from £(　　) to £(　　).

5) She has worked for over (　　) years and signed an agreement to have a pension payable at age (　　) at final salary.

解答

1) Manchester drivers pay average annual insurance premiums of £(563) compared with a national average of £(406).
   [マンチェスターの運転手は、全国平均406ポンドに対し、年間で平均563ポンドの保険料を支払っている]

2) They already paid $(7.2) M of the $(20) M total insurance premiums so far.
   [合計2,000万ドルの保険料のうち、彼らが現在までに支払っているのは720万ドルだ]

3) An agreement has been reached in a lawsuit involving his $(10) MM {£(7) MM} life insurance policy.
   [彼の1,000万ドル（700万ポンド）の生命保険にからんだ訴訟で、1つの合意がなされた]

4) They want the government to increase the basic state pension from £(85) to £(111).
   ［彼らは政府に対して、基本的な国民年金を85ポンドから111ポンドに引き上げてほしいと思っている］

5) She has worked for over (27) years and signed an agreement to have a pension payable at age (60) at final salary.
   ［彼女は、27年以上仕事をしており、60歳から最終給与に基づく年金を支給されるという同意書にサインをしていた］

🎧 TRACK 41

2 CDから流れてくる日本語を聴き、即座に英語に直して発話してください。（＊日本語の後ポーズがあって、その後すぐに英語が流れます）

1)   2)
3)

【解答】

1) 事業主負担3割　　　　　　employer's contribution 30%
2) 5万ポンドを超える損害　　damage in excess of £50,000
3) 700万ドルの生命保険証券　a $7 M life insurance policy

3 以下の日本語を英語に直して発話してください。　🎧 TRACK 42

1) 私の保険の掛金は、1ヵ月12,000円だ。

2) 彼は、妻に1億5,000万円の生命保険を掛けた。

3) 保険料に3,000ポンドかかる。

【解答】

1) I pay ¥12,000 a month as an insurance premium.
2) He took out a ¥150 million life insurance policy on his wife.
3) The insurance premium costs £3,000.

4 通信・情報・IT

Communication、Information、Information Technology

住所、郵便、電話　Address、Mail、Telephone

住　所

住　所

- 〒 105-0011 東京都港区芝公園 4-2-8
  (4-2-8 Shibakoen Minato-ku, Tokyo 105-0011 Japan)
- 350 5th Ave New York, NY 10018, USA
  (Three fifty Fifth Avenue, New York New York, one oh oh one eight USA)

　　＊欧米の住所は、「番地→通り→都市→州（など）→国」の順番に表示します。番地の「-」は、ダッシュかハイフンと読みます。

　　＊郵便番号の読み方は、以下の「郵便番号」の欄を参照してください。

部屋番号

□ 1103	eleven oh three	
□ 2795	twenty-seven ninety-five	
□ 864	eight six four、eight sixty-four	
□ 3 号棟 602 号室	Room 602 in Building 3	(six oh two)
□ 12 号室	Apt 12	(apartment twelve)
□ 47 番	#47	(number forty-seven)

郵　便

郵便番号

- 7 桁の郵便番号　　seven-digit postal code
- 5 桁の郵便番号　　five-digit zip code

- ☐ 品川郵便局私書箱14号　　Shinagawa P.O.Box 14
- ☐ 〒106-0031　　　　　　（one oh / zero six, oh / zero oh / zero three one）
- ☐ ビバリーヒルズ90210　　Beverly Hills 90210　　（nine oh two one oh）

電話

国番号、局番

- ☐ 国番号　　　country code、international call prefix
- ☐ 市外局番　　area code
- ☐ 局番なし　　no prefix

電話番号

- ☐ 03-1234-5678
  zero / oh three, one two three four, five six seven eight
  ＊通常、数字を1つ1つ読みます。日本語では「-」の部分を「の」と読むことが多いですが、英語では何も言わずに、ひと息間を置きます。
- ☐ (212) 890-4321
  two one two, eight nine zero / oh, four three two one
- ☐ 3335　　three three three five、thirty-three thirty-five、triple three five
- ☐ 4900　　four nine oh oh、forty-nine hundred、four nine double zero / oh
- ☐ 5000　　five thousand
- ☐ 0120　　zero one two zero、oh one two oh
- ☐ 1-800　　one eight hundred
  ＊日本の通話料無料の番号は0120、0800などで始まりますが、アメリカは1-800です。800のほかにも866、877、888があります。
- ☐ 内線27　　extension 27　　（twenty-seven）

特殊番号

- 911　nine one one
  *アメリカの緊急番号です。日本は、119（救急、消防）、110（警察）です。イギリスでは、999、EU 圏内の共通緊急番号は、112 です。
- 411　four one one
  *アメリカの directory assistance（電話番号案内）の番号です。日本は、104 です。

放送、情報技術　Broadcast、Information technology

テレビ、ラジオ

チャンネル、番組

- 4 チャンネル　　　　　　　　　　Channel 4
- 30 の衛星放送チャンネル　　　　　30 satellite channels
- 90 分のテレビ番組　　　　　　　　90-minute television show
- 5 つの番組　　　　　　　　　　　5 programs / programmes
- 米軍ネットワーク、イーグル 810　　AFN Eagle 810　　（eight ten）
  　　　　　　　　　　　　　　　　＊ AFN = American Forces Network

放送時間

- 放送時間：午前 9 時から 9 時半
  Airtime / Broadcast / Timeslot: 9:00 am to 9:30am

周波数

- ラジオチャイナ 1557 キロヘルツ
  Radio China 1557 kHz　（fifteen fifty-seven kilohertz）
  　＊ kHz = kilohertz
- 東京 FM 80.0 メガヘルツ
  TOKYO FM 80.0MHz　（eighty point zero megahertz）
  　＊ MHz = megahertz

視聴率

- 視聴率 14.1%　　audience rating 14.1%

コンピュータ

ビット

* ビットはコンピュータが扱う情報の最小単位です。
- ☐ 32 ビットのパソコン　　　　　32-bit personal computer
- ☐ ウィンドウズ・ビスタ 64 ビット　　Windows Vista 64-Bit
- ☐ 56 キロビット/秒モデム　　56 kbps modem　　* kbps = kilobit per second

バイト

* バイトは、コンピュータ関連の情報量を表す単位です。
- ☐ 1 バイト　　　　　1 byte = 8 bits
- ☐ 1 キロバイト　　　1 kB = 1,024 bytes　　* kB = kilobyte
- ☐ 1 メガバイト　　　1 MB = 1,024 kB　　　* MB = megabyte
- ☐ 1 ギガバイト　　　1 GB = 1,024 MB　　　* GB = gigabyte

CPU (Central Processing Unit)

* CPU は、機器制御や数値計算、情報処理をおこなうコンピュータの中心的な部品です。
- ☐ 400 メガヘルツの CPU　　400 MHz CPU　　* MHz = megahertz

メモリ

- ☐ 64 メガバイトのメモリ　　　　　64 MB of memory　　* MB = megabyte
- ☐ 20 メガバイトの空きメモリ　　　20 MB of free memory
- ☐ 8 ギガバイトのメモリースティック　8 GB memory stick　　* GB = gigabyte

ハードディスク

- ☐ 500 ギガバイトのハードディスク　　500 GB hard disc drive

ソフトウエア

- □ ウィンドウズ 2000　　Windows 2000
- □ アイフォン 2.0　　　　iPhone 2.0
- □ アイチューン 7.7　　　iTunes 7.7

～倍速

- □ 倍速　　　　　　　　double / dual-speed
- □ 4 倍速　　　　　　　4X speed　　　　（four times speed）
- □ 8 倍速　　　　　　　8X speed　　　　（eight times speed）
- □ 20 倍速 CD-ROM　　20X CD-ROM　（twenty times speed）

新聞、雑誌、書籍　Newspapers、Magazines、Books

新聞、雑誌、書籍

出版、発行、販売 / 発行部数

☐ Her first novel was published in 1978.
　［彼女の最初の小説は、1978年に出版された］
☐ Japanese journals issued in 2008 are now available.
　［2008年に発行された日本語の新聞は、現在入手可能である］
☐ Daily sales: only 25,469 copies
　［1日の販売部数：わずか25,469部］
☐ The newspaper circulation has dropped 11.3 percent since 1984.
　［その新聞の発行部数は、1984年以来11.3％落ちている］

購読、購読者数

☐ 6ヵ月間の定期購読　　　6-month subscription
☐ 1日の購読者数120万人　daily circulation of 1.2 million people
☐ 300万の購読者数　　　　readership of 3 million

連　載

☐ 16回連載　　　　　　　16 installments
☐ 10回シリーズの第1回　the first installment of a ten-part series
☐ 連載4コマ漫画　　　　　a series of a four-frame comic（strip）/ manga

部、版、巻、号、冊

☐ 10万部の売上げ　　　　sales of 100,000 copies
☐ 初版第2刷　　　　　　　the second printing of the first edition
☐ 第3刷　　　　　　　　　the third printing
☐ 全10巻セット　　　　　ten-volume set
☐ 5月1日号　　　　　　　issue for May 1
☐ 1冊の値段は4ドル56セントだ。　The price per issue is $4.56.

面、ページ

- [ ] 1面   the front page
- [ ] 三面記事   city / local news
- [ ] 第35面   p. 35
- [ ] 18ページ参照   See p. 18
- [ ] 12ページ分の広告   12 pages of ads

段落、段、章、節

- [ ] 第4段落   the fourth paragraph
- [ ] 第2段組   the second column
- [ ] 3段分   three columns
- [ ] 第1章   Chapter 1（chapter one / the first chapter）
- [ ] 第5節   Section 5

図、表、グラフ

- [ ] 第3図   Fig. 3（figure three）
- [ ] 表2   Table 2
- [ ] グラフ5   Graph 5

折り込み

- [ ] 8ページの折り込み付録   8-page pullout supplement
- [ ] 8ページの折り込み   eight-page foldout

その他

- [ ] 国際標準図書番号   ISBN（= International Standard Book Number）
- [ ] 目次   table of contents
- [ ] 索引   index
- [ ] 巻末   end
- [ ] 署名記事   article with a byline、attributed article

15 通信、情報、IT・徹底トレーニング

1 CDから流れてくる英文を聴き、カッコの部分を書き取ってください。

1) On the south side is the Peach Hotel {( ) Main Street; ( )-( )-( )}.

2) The book became the publisher's fastest-selling hardcover fiction, selling ( ) copies in its first ( ) days of publication.

3) Daily sales fell ( )% to ( ) copies.

4) You can watch BBC News ( ) on freeview channel ( ), satellite channel ( ), and cable channels ( ), ( ) or ( ).

5) Is the maximum memory that you can attain ( ) MB or ( ) MB?

6) The program was watched by ( ) million viewers, a rise of ( )% over the initially reported figure.

7) Located at ( ) Mill Street {Route ( )}, Rhinebeck, {( ) ( )-( )}, Lunch for ( ), about $( ).

8) Gift subscription terms: U.S., Canada, International, ( ) year {( ) issues}, $( ), $( ), $( ). ( ) years {( ) issues}, $( ), $( ), $( ).

9) Thanks to their grid computing network, more than ( ) processors at ( ) institutes around the world are linked together.

10) We are on the air Sundays from ( ) to ( ) p.m. at ( ) kHz on your AM dial.

解 答

1) On the south side is the Peach Hotel {(524) Main Street; (410)-(231)-(3336)}.
   [南側にピーチホテル（メイン通り524、電話は410-231-3336）がある]

2) The book became the publisher's fastest-selling hardcover fiction, selling (44,093) copies in its first (four) days of publication.
   [その本は、発売開始から4日間で44,093冊を売上げ、出版社始まって以来最速で売れたハードカバーの小説となった]

3) Daily sales fell (7)% to (34,439,713) copies.
   [1日の販売部数は7%落ちて、34,439,713部になった]

4) You can watch BBC News (24) on freeview channel (80), satellite channel (507), and cable channels (10), (125) or (610).
   [BBCニュース24は、フリービューチャンネル80、衛星チャンネル507、ケーブルチャンネル10、125か610で観ることができる]

5) Is the maximum memory that you can attain (49) MB or (50) MB?
   [入手可能な、容量が最大のメモリーは、49メガバイト（のメディア）か、それとも50メガバイトですか]

6) The program was watched by (1.98) million viewers, a rise of (10)% over the initially reported figure.
   [そのプログラムは、198万人の人が見たが、それは最初に報告された数字を10%上回った]

7) Located at (6384) Mill Street {Route (9)}, Rhinebeck, {(845) (876)-(2749)}, Lunch for (two), about $(50).
   [ラインベック：所在地、ミル通り6384（国道9）、電話845-876-2749、ランチ2人で約50ドル]

8) Gift subscription terms: U.S., Canada, International, (1) year {(4) issues}, $(19.97), $(27.97), $(31.97). (2) years {(8) issues}, $(34.97), $(50.97), $(58.97).
   [ギフト用の定期購読条件：アメリカ、カナダ、海外。1年間（4冊）、19.97ドル、27.97ドル、31.97ドル。2年間（8冊）、34.97ドル、50.97ドル、58.97ドル]

9) Thanks to their grid computing network, more than (100,000) processors at (140) institutes around the world are linked together.

[彼らのグリッド・コンピューティングのおかげで、世界全体で140ヵ所の施設にある10万台以上のプロセッサーがつながっている]

＊グリッド・コンピューティングは、ネットワークを介して複数のコンピュータを結び、1台のコンピュータのように利用する技術のことです。

10) We are on the air Sundays from (2:00) to (3:00) p.m. at (738) kHz on your AM dial.

[毎週日曜日、午後2時から3時、AM738キロヘルツでお届けします]

5 交通
Transportation

飛行機、自動車、電車　Airplanes、Automobiles、Trains

飛行機

飛行機

- □ ボーイング 747　　　　Boeing 747　　　　　　（seven forty-seven）
- □ エアバス A321　　　　Airbus A 321　　　　　（three twenty-one）
- □ 日本航空 272 便　　　 JL / JAL 272　　　　　 （two seventy-two）
- □ 4502 便　　　　　　　Flight number 4502　　（forty-five oh two）
- □ 座席番号 18 F　　　　Seat 18 F　　　　　　 （eighteen）

空　港

- □ ヒースロー空港ターミナル 4　　Heathrow Airport Terminal 4
- □ 搭乗口 56　　　　　　　　　　Gate 56　　　（fifty-six）
- □ 荷物制限 32 キログラム　　　　baggage allowance 32 kg

自動車

車　種

- □ 6 人乗りの電気自動車　　　six-seater electric car
- □ 4 ドアの車　　　　　　　　four-door car

エンジン、排気量、走行距離、燃費、CO_2 排出量

- □ 8 気筒エンジン　　　　　　　　　　8-cylinder engine
- □ 排気量 1,000cc のエンジン　　　　 engine size of 1,000 cc
- □ 排気量 2,400cc のディーゼルエンジン　2,400-cc diesel engine

☐ 走行距離計表示 26,284 マイル	odometer reading of 26,284 miles
☐ 燃費、1リットルあたり 38 キロメートル	fuel efficiency of 38 km / l
☐ CO_2 排出量、1キロメートルあたり 61 グラム	CO_2 emissions: 61 g / km

5 交通

道 路

☐ 国道1号線	Route 1
☐ 一方通行	one-way traffic / street
☐ 三叉路	three-way intersection
☐ ～は7キロメートルの渋滞だ	～ is backed up for 7 km
☐ 制限速度（時速）50 マイル	speed limit 50、50-mph speed limit
☐ 普通車	ordinary / standard-sized vehicle
☐ 二軸車	two-axle vehicle
☐ 普通車の通行料金：1,000 円	Toll for ordinary vehicle: 1,000 yen

電 車

電車、列車

☐ 15両編成の列車	fifteen-coach / fifteen-car train
☐ 前部4車両	first 4 coaches / cars
☐ 後部6車両	rear 6 coaches / cars
☐ 1等車	first-class car / coach / carriage
☐ 7時8分発の電車	the 7:08 train
☐ 2ドルの均一料金	flat rate of two dollars

駅

☐ 2駅乗り越す	go 2 stops beyond one's destination
☐ 3番ホーム	platform / track 3

その他

☐ 片道（切符）	one way (ticket)（米）、single (ticket)（英）
☐ 往復（切符）	round trip (ticket)（米）、return (ticket)（英）

- ☐ 6日間有効　　　　valid / good for 6 days
- ☐ 3ヵ月の通勤定期　three-month commuter pass
- ☐ 地下鉄　　　　　　subway（米）、underground / tube（英）、metro（欧）
- ☐ 地下道　　　　　　underground / underpass（米）、subway（英）

TRACK 44

16 交通・徹底トレーニング

1 CDから流れてくる英文を聴き、カッコの部分を書き取ってください。

1) The rear-wheel-drive M-(　) convertible, with its (　)-liter, (　)-horsepower, V-(　) engine, uses premium fuel at a rate that translates to (　) miles per gallon in the city and (　) miles per gallon on the highway.

2) Shuttle Coach to London. Fare : £(　) Single, £(　) Return. {Children (　)-(　) Half Price}

3) The airline company allows you (　) carry-on, and the size limit is strict: weight: (　) kg, length: (　) cm, height: (　) cm, depth: (　) cm {(　) lbs., (　) long, (　) high, (　) wide)}.

4) The taxi fare starts at (　) yen for up to (　) km, and (　) yen is added for every (　) m. From late night to early morning {(　) pm to (　) am} the fare is increased by (　)%.

5) Flight number: AA (　), Departs: (　), From: Tokyo (NRT), Arrives: (　), To: Dallas / Fort Worth (DFW), Flight time: (　) hrs (　) min

解 答

1) The rear-wheel-drive M-(6) convertible, with its (5)-liter, (500)-horsepower, V-(10) engine, uses premium fuel at a rate that translates to (11) miles per gallon in the city and (17) miles per gallon on the highway.
　　[後輪駆動のM-6コンバーチブルは、5リッター、500馬力のV-10エンジンを搭載し、市街地では1ガロンあたり11マイル、高速道路では17マイルの燃費で、プレミアムガソリン仕様である]

2) Shuttle Coach to London. Fare : £(10.00) Single, £(17.00) Return. {Children (3)-(15) Half Price}
   [ロンドン行きシャトルバス。料金：片道 10 ポンド、往復 17 ポンド（3 歳から 15 歳までの子ども半額）]
   ＊coach には、電車の「車両」以外に、「バス」の意味があります。

3) The airline company allows you (one) carry-on, and the size limit is strict: weight: (5) kg, length: (55) cm, height: (25) cm, depth: (35) cm {(11) lbs., (21.5") long, (10") high, (13.5") wide}.
   [その航空会社では、機内に持ち込める手荷物は 1 つのみ。サイズは厳格に、重さ 5 キログラム、長さ 55 センチメートル、高さ 25 センチメートル、幅 35 センチメートル（11 ポンド、21.5 インチ、10 インチ、13.5 インチ）までと決められている]

4) The taxi fare starts at (710) yen for up to (2) km, and (90) yen is added for every (288) m. From late night to early morning {(11) pm to (5) am} the fare is increased by (20)%.
   [タクシー料金は、2 キロメートルまで 710 円、そして 288 メートルごとに 90 円加算される。深夜から早朝（午後 11 時から午前 5 時まで）は、2 割増しになる]

5) Flight number: AA (176), Departs: (12:05), From: Tokyo (NRT), Arrives: (09:25), To: Dallas / Fort Worth (DFW), Flight time: (11) hrs (20) min
   [便名：AA176、出発時刻：12 時 5 分、出発地：東京（成田）、到着時刻：9 時 25 分、到着地：ダラス / フォートウォース、飛行時間：11 時間 20 分]

6 日常の数字
Daily Life

食料品、料理　Food and Drink、Cooking

食料品

乳製品、卵

- ☐ 牛乳1パック（大）　　　　　　a carton of milk、milk carton
- ☐ 紙パック入り牛乳1つ（中、小）　a package / packet of milk
- ☐ 卵1パック　　　　　　　　　　a carton / case of eggs
- ☐ チーズ1切れ　　　　　　　　　a piece / slice of cheese

肉、魚、豆腐

- ☐ 肉1切れ / 1片　　　　　a piece of meat
- ☐ ベーコン薄切り1枚　　　a slice of bacon
- ☐ 鶏肉1ポンド　　　　　　a pound of chicken
- ☐ 牛の挽肉300グラム　　　300 grams of ground beef
- ☐ 1枚の厚切りの牛肉　　　a slab of beef
- ☐ 1塊の豚肉　　　　　　　a cut of pork
- ☐ 1匹の魚　　　　　　　　a piece of fish
- ☐ サケの切り身3枚　　　　three pieces of salmon
- ☐ 豆腐1丁　　　　　　　　a piece / cake of tofu

野菜、果物

- ☐ ジャガイモ1袋　　　a bag of potatoes
- ☐ ホウレン草1束　　　a bundle of spinach
- ☐ キャベツ1株　　　　a head of cabbage
- ☐ トウモロコシ1本　　an ear of corn
- ☐ ニンニク1片　　　　a clove of garlic

109

☐ トマト1山	a pile of tomatoes
☐ バナナ1房	a bunch of bananas
☐ ミカンの1房	a section / segment of tangerine

ご飯、パン類

☐ ご飯1膳（杯）	a bowl of rice
☐ パン1枚	a slice of bread
☐ パン1斤	a loaf of bread

飲　料

☐ コーヒー1杯	a cup of coffee
☐ ジュース1杯	a glass of juice
☐ 缶ビール6缶パック	a six-pack of beer
☐ ワイン1瓶	a bottle of wine
☐ アルコール度数5%	alcohol content 5%
☐ 30年もののウイスキー	a 30-year-old whiskey
☐ 1995年もののメルロー	a '95 Merlot

＊19（nineteen）は、通常、省略します。

菓　子

☐ 板チョコ1枚	a tablet / bar of chocolate / a chocolate bar
☐ クッキー1箱	a box of cookies
☐ ポテトチップス1袋	a bag of chips / crisps
☐ 1すくいのアイスクリーム	a scoop of ice cream
☐ 1カップのアイスクリーム	a cup of ice cream

料理

調味料

- ☐ 味噌大さじ 1 杯　　a tablespoon of miso / soybean paste
- ☐ 砂糖小さじ 1 杯　　a teaspoon of sugar
- ☐ 塩 1 つまみ　　　　a pinch of salt
- ☐ 胡椒 1 ふり　　　　a dash of pepper
- ☐ コンソメ 1 個　　　a lump / cube of consommé / bouillon
- ☐ バター 1 キューブ　a cube of butter
- ☐ 小麦粉 1 カップ　　a cup of flour

17 食料品、料理・徹底トレーニング

1 CDから流れてくる英文を聴き、カッコの部分を書き取ってください。

1) A loaf of bread, $( ); a pint of beer, $( ); a pint of milk, $( ).

2) Use ( ) g risotto rice, and the finely grated zest of ( ) unwaxed lemons.

3) The ( ) were charged with making a ( )-course meal for ( ) with a $( ) budget.

4) Super Diet balances a ratio of ( )% complex carbohydrates, ( )% lean protein and ( )% favorable fats for perfectly balanced nutrition that helps you lose weight.

5) In recent years the alcohol content of standard lager has risen from ( )% to ( )% and wine from ( )% to ( )%.

6) Tasters sampling a bottle of ( )-century wine which lay buried for more than ( ) years declared it better than expected.

7) Ingredients: ( ) pheasant breasts, boned & skinned; ( ) shallots, finely chopped; ( ) garlic cloves, crushed; ( ) ml chicken stock

8) Wine and cream sauce: ( ) ml {( ) tablespoons} wine, ( ) ml {( ) cup} half-and-half, and ( ) ml {( ) cup} chicken stock.

9) Start with ( ) ml vegetable stock, ( ) g unsalted butter, and ( ) tablespoon olive oil.

10) Cut eight discs of sponge (　　) cm wide and (　　) cm thick and place them inside the rings on a buttered baking sheet, (　　) cm apart.

解答

1) A loaf of bread, $(2.50); a pint of beer, $(3); a pint of milk, $(0.43).
   [パン1斤2ドル50セント、ビール1パイント3ドル、牛乳1パイント43セント]

2) Use (275) g risotto rice, and the finely grated zest of (2) unwaxed lemons.
   [リゾット用米275グラム、レモン（ノンワックス）の皮2個分、細かくすりおろしたもの]

3) The (two) were charged with making a (three)-course meal for (two) with a $(20) budget.
   [その2人は20ドルの予算で、2人分の3品のコース料理を作ることを任された]

4) Super Diet balances a ratio of (40)% complex carbohydrates, (30)% lean protein and (30)% favorable fats for perfectly balanced nutrition that helps you lose weight.
   [スーパーダイエットは、40％の複合炭水化物、30％の低カロリーたんぱく質、30％の良質な脂肪という理想の栄養バランスで、あなたのダイエットをお手伝いします]

5) In recent years the alcohol content of standard lager has risen from (3.5)% to (4.5)% and wine from (10)% to (13)%.
   [近年、スタンダードラガー（ビール）のアルコール度数が3.5％から4.5％へ、そしてワインが10％から13％へ上がった]

6) Tasters sampling a bottle of (17th)-century wine which lay buried for more than (300) years declared it better than expected.
   [300年以上寝かせていた、17世紀のワインを試飲したテイスターたちは、予想していたよりもおいしいと言った]

7) Ingredients: (4) pheasant breasts, boned & skinned; (8) shallots, finely chopped; (2) garlic cloves, crushed; (100) ml chicken stock
   [材料：キジ胸肉4切れ、骨と皮を取り除いたもの。エシャロット8個、みじん切り。ニンニク2片、つぶしたもの。チキンストック、100ミリリットル]

8) Wine and cream sauce: (30) ml {(two) tablespoons} wine, (60) ml {(1/4) cup} half-and-half, and (120) ml {(1/2) cup} chicken stock.
   [ワインクリームソース：30 ミリリットル（大さじ 2 杯）のワインと 60 ミリリットル（1/4 カップ）のハーフアンドハーフ。120 ミリリットル（1/2 カップ）のチキンストック]
   ＊half-and-half ＝クリームに同量のミルクを加えたもの。

9) Start with (900) ml vegetable stock, (50) g unsalted butter, and (1) tablespoon olive oil.
   [野菜スープストック 900 ミリリットル、無塩バター 50 グラム、オリーブオイル大さじ 1 杯を、まずあわせます]

10) Cut eight discs of sponge (8) cm wide and (1/2) cm thick and place them inside the rings on a buttered baking sheet, (6-7) cm apart.
    [スポンジを幅 8 センチメートル、厚さ 0.5 センチメートルの円状に 8 枚カットし、リング型に入れてバターを塗った天板に置く。6 〜 7 センチメートルの間隔をあけること]

TRACK 46

2 CD から流れてくる日本語を聴き、即座に英語に直して発話してください。（＊日本語の後ポーズがあって、その後すぐに英語が流れます）

1)　　　　　　　　　　　　2)
3)　　　　　　　　　　　　4)
5)

解 答

1) バター大さじ 1 杯　　　　　　1 Tbsp. butter　　＊Tbsp. = tablespoon
2) おかず 5 品の夕食　　　　　　a five-course dinner
3) 賞味期限：2010 年 1 月 31 日　　Best before: Jan. 31, 2010
4) 6 枚の取り分け皿　　　　　　six serving plates
5) 25%以上のアルコール度数　　an alcohol content of over 25 percent

3 以下の日本語を英語に直して発話してください。　　**TRACK 47**

1) 41%の高いカカオ含有率

2) パルメザンチーズ 100 グラム、おろしたてのもの

3) ボールにクスクスを入れて 150 ミリリットルの水を振りかける。

4) 魚とエビを加えて、2 分間軽く茹でる。

5) 小麦粉―3 カップ 1 ドル 50 セント、そして肉は―小さい 1 片が 1 ドルする。

解 答

1) High 41% cacao content
2) 100g of parmesan cheese, freshly grated
3) Tip the couscous into a bowl and sprinkle with 150 ml of water.
4) Add the fish and prawns, and poach gently for 2 minutes.
5) Flour ― three cups for $1.50, and meat ― a small slice costs $1.

医療、厚生　Medicine、Health and Welfare

医療、厚生

平熱、体温

☐ His normal body temperature is 37°C.
　　［彼の平熱は（摂氏）37度だ］
☐ Her body temperature has fallen to 88°F.
　　［彼女の体温は（華氏）88度まで下がった］

血　圧

☐ Normal blood pressure is 120 / 80 or less.
　　［正常な血圧は、上は120、下は80かそれ以下である］
　　＊読み方は、120 over 80。
　　＊血圧の単位は、mmHg（= millimeters of mercury）。

脈拍数、心拍数

☐ She had a pulse rate of 140 when it should have been 80.
　　［彼女の脈拍数は、80であるべきところ140もあった］
☐ He had a heart rate of 180 beats per minute ― three times above what is considered normal.
　　［彼の心拍数は1分間に180だった。それは、正常とされる値の3倍だった］

視　力

☐ I have 20 / 20 vision so I don't need glasses.
　　［私の視力は20 / 20なので、眼鏡は必要ない］
　　　＊20 / 20　twenty-twenty vision
　　　＊20フィート離れた指標20の文字（= 1/3インチ径の文字）を識別できる視力。日本の視力1.0に相当します。
☐ My naked vision is 20 / 40 (= 0.5).
　　［私の裸眼視力は、20 / 40 (= 0.5) だ］

- ☐ I have 0.3 vision in my right eye, and 0.1 in my left.
    ［私の右目の視力は 0.3 で、左目は 0.1 だ］

コレステロール値

- ☐ The risk of heart attack more than doubles when the total cholesterol level approaches 300 mg/dL.
    ［心臓発作をおこすリスクは、コレステロール値が 300mg/dL に近づくと 2 倍以上になる］
        * mg/dL = milligram/deciliter
- ☐ I've been trying to reduce my cholesterol count from 300 down to 167.
    ［私は自分のコレステロール値を、300 から 167 まで下げるように努力中である］

血糖値

- ☐ A normal blood sugar level after an oral glucose tolerance test is lower than 140 mg/dL.
    ［経口ブドウ糖負荷試験後の、正常な血糖値は 140mg/dL 以下である］
- ☐ Diabetes is typically diagnosed when fasting blood glucose levels are 126 mg/dL or higher.
    ［通常、空腹時の血糖値が 126mg/dL 以上のときに糖尿病と診断される］

体脂肪率

- ☐ The average person has between 17 and 25% body fat percentage / rate.
    ［平均的な人の体脂肪率は、17 から 25％の間である］

体格指数（BMI）

- ☐ BMI Categories: Obesity = BMI of 30 or greater
    ［体格指数カテゴリー：肥満＝ BMI 30 以上］
        BMI = body-mass index

妊娠、出産

- The baby was due on 7 September.
    [赤ちゃんの誕生予定日は、9月7日だった]
- She is four and a half months pregnant.
    [彼女は、妊娠4ヵ月半である]
- Pre-natal scans are no longer offered automatically in the 35th week of pregnancy.
    [産前検査は、今では妊娠第35週に自動的に実施されることはない]
    ＊日本では、妊娠期間を「十月十日（とつきとおか）」といって約10ヵ月としていますが、英語圏では9ヵ月です。これは1ヵ月の概念が違うためです（日本＝4週間＝28日、英語圏＝30〜31日）。したがって、「臨月」は英語でnine monthsといいます。
- The 2,800g baby was delivered by a midwife at midnight.
    [2,800グラムの赤ちゃんが、助産師によって真夜中に取り上げられた]

薬

- A single dose of the liquid dilution homeopathic remedy is usually 10 to 20 drops.
    [ホメオパシー薬品の希釈液の1回の服用量は、通常10から20滴だ]
    ＊homeopathy　ホメオパシー　同種療法、同毒療法
- Gradually, he increased the daily dosage to a maximum of 270mg.
    [徐々に、彼は1日の服用量を、最大限の270ミリグラムまで増やした]
- Cough suppressant, grape-flavored liquid: 2 teaspoons every 12 hours, not to exceed 4 teaspoons in 24 hours.
    [せき止め、グレープ味の水薬：12時間おきに小さじ2杯、24時間以内に小さじ4杯を超えないこと]

〈その他の医薬品〉

- 錠剤　　pill、tablet、caplet
- 粉薬　　powdered medicine
- 目薬　　eye-drops
- 貼り薬　adhesive skin patch
- 軟膏　　ointment

- ☐ 栄養剤　　nutritional supplement
- ☐ 漢方薬　　Chinese herbal madicine

その他

- ☐ メタボリック症候群　　　　metabolic syndrome
- ☐ 生活習慣病（成人病）　　　lifestyle-related disease（adult disease）
- ☐ SPF値、日焼け防止指数　　SPF = sun protection factor
- ☐ 歯周病　　　　　　　　　　gum disease

18 医療、厚生・徹底トレーニング

1 CDから流れてくる英文を聴き、カッコの部分を書き取ってください。

1) I was shocked to find my blood oxygen level had dropped to (　　) percent — it is normally around (　　).

2) (　　) caplets. (　　) caplets contain (　　) mg beta-sitosterol, (　) mg of beta-glucan and (　　) mg of soy isoflavones. Each bottle contains a (　　)-month supply.

3) Astaxanthin has been scientifically proven to be (　　) times more effective as an antioxidant than carotene and (　　)-(　　) times more effective than vitamin E.

4) (　　) mg × (　　) capsules. Each capsule contains (　　) mg of fresh aloe gel.

5) In the last (　　) weeks, my vision has gone from (　　) to (　　).

6) Most capsule forms of green tea extract contain (　　)-(　　)% polyphenols.

7) Dosage: (　　) drops in some water (　　) a day before meals. Treatment Period: (　　) days, can vary slightly depending upon the severity of the condition.

8) About (　　) in (　　) adults over age (　　) has blood pressure greater than (　　).

9) My doctor told me my body fat rate was about (　　)% when it should ideally be between (　　)% and (　　)%.

10) The women studied were between the ages of (　) and (　) and were examined between the (　) and (　) weeks of pregnancy.

解 答

1) I was shocked to find my blood oxygen level had dropped to (89) percent — it is normally around (100).
　　[驚いたことに、私の血中酸素濃度が89％まで下がってしまっていた。通常は100前後なのに]

2) (Sixty) caplets. (Two) caplets contain (300) mg beta-sitosterol, (200) mg of beta-glucan and (40) mg of soy isoflavones. Each bottle contains a (one)-month supply.
　　[60錠入り。2錠中にβ-シトステロール300ミリグラム、β-グルカン200ミリグラム、大豆イソフラボン40ミリグラム含有。1瓶は1ヵ月分に相当]

3) Astaxanthin has been scientifically proven to be (10) times more effective as an antioxidant than carotene and (100)-(500) times more effective than vitamin E.
　　[アスタキサンチンは、カロテンの10倍、ビタミンEの100～500倍効果的な抗酸化物質であると、科学的に証明された]

4) (100) mg × (60) capsules. Each capsule contains (20) mg of fresh aloe gel.
　　[100ミリグラム、60カプセル入り。1カプセルにつき、生のアロエゲル20ミリグラムを含む]

5) In the last (six) weeks, my vision has gone from (20 / 20) to (20 / 50).
　　[この6週間で、私の視力は20 / 20から20 / 50になった]

6) Most capsule forms of green tea extract contain (40)-(50)％ polyphenols.
　　[大抵のカプセル型の緑茶抽出液には、40～50％のポリフェノールが含まれる]

7) Dosage: (20) drops in some water (twice) a day before meals. Treatment Period: (80) days, can vary slightly depending upon the severity of the condition.
　　[用量：20滴を少量の水に溶かし、食前に1日2回。服用期間：80日―症状の程度によって多少前後する]

8) About (one) in (five) adults over age (40) has blood pressure greater than (140 / 85).
   [40歳以上の大人の、約5人に1人の血圧は、140 / 85を超える]

9) My doctor told me my body fat rate was about (35)% when it should ideally be between (20)% and (24)%.
   [私の主治医は、理想的な体脂肪率は20〜24%であるべきなのに、私の体脂肪率は約35%だと告げた]

10) The women studied were between the ages of (20) and (35) and were examined between the (36th) and (38th) weeks of pregnancy.
    [調査対象は、20〜35歳の女性で、そのうち第36〜38週の妊婦が検査を受けた]

TRACK 49

2 CDから流れてくる日本語を聴き、即座に英語に直して発話してください。（＊日本語の後ポーズがあって、その後すぐに英語が流れます）

1)
2)
3)
4)
5)

解答

1) 500ミリグラム、60カプセル入り　　　　　　　500 mg × 60 capsules
2) SPF15度の日焼け止めクリーム　　　　　　　SPF 15 + sunscreen
3) 10万件の皮膚がんの症例　　　　　　　　100,000 cases of skin cancer
4) 心拍数1分間に140　　　　　　　heart rate of 140 beats per minute
5) 本当のコエンザイムQ10を1%含んだクリーム
　　　　　　　　　　　　　　　the cream with an actual 1% CoQ 10

3 以下の日本語を英語に直して発話してください。　TRACK 50

1) 集中的な運動で、心拍数が1分間に180回までに上がった。

2) 回復期のアルコール依存症患者で、たばこを以前1日に1箱吸っていた者

3) 私は、5ヵ月で5ポンド減量した。

4) 彼女は、妊娠3ヵ月であると報告されている。

5) 彼の体温が、42度まで上がった。

[解 答]

1) I raised my heart rate to 180 bpm through intensive exercise.
     bpm = beats per minute　拍 / 分
2) a recovering alcoholic and former pack-a-day smoker
3) I lost 5 pounds in 5 months.
4) She is reported to be three months pregnant.
5) His body temperature hit 42°C.

電気器具 / 設備、カメラ、写真　Electric Appliances、Camera、Photography

電気器具 / 設備

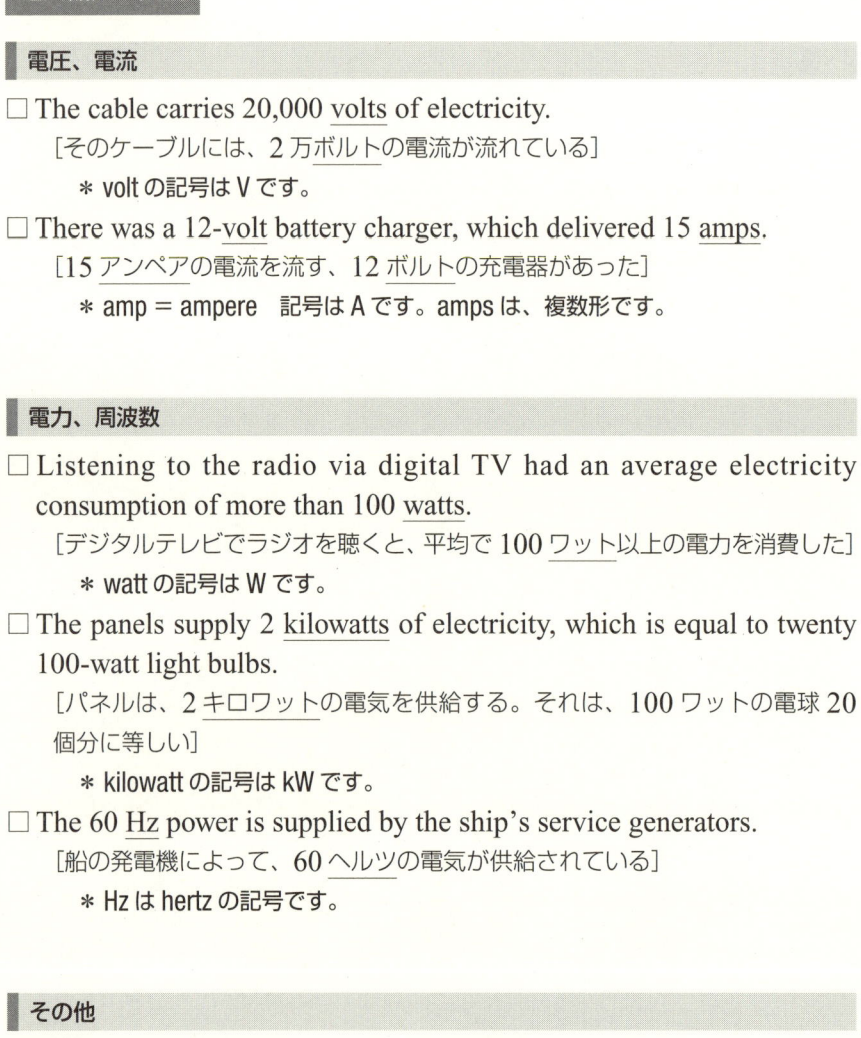

電圧、電流

□ The cable carries 20,000 volts of electricity.
　　［そのケーブルには、2 万ボルトの電流が流れている］
　　　＊ volt の記号は V です。

□ There was a 12-volt battery charger, which delivered 15 amps.
　　［15 アンペアの電流を流す、12 ボルトの充電器があった］
　　　＊ amp = ampere　記号は A です。amps は、複数形です。

電力、周波数

□ Listening to the radio via digital TV had an average electricity consumption of more than 100 watts.
　　［デジタルテレビでラジオを聴くと、平均で 100 ワット以上の電力を消費した］
　　　＊ watt の記号は W です。

□ The panels supply 2 kilowatts of electricity, which is equal to twenty 100-watt light bulbs.
　　［パネルは、2 キロワットの電気を供給する。それは、100 ワットの電球 20 個分に等しい］
　　　＊ kilowatt の記号は kW です。

□ The 60 Hz power is supplied by the ship's service generators.
　　［船の発電機によって、60 ヘルツの電気が供給されている］
　　　＊ Hz は hertz の記号です。

その他

□（壁に取り付けられた）コンセント　　　outlet
□ 変圧器　　　　　　　　　　　　　　　electric transformer
□ 40 ワットの白熱電球　　　　　　　　　40-watt incandescent light bulb
□ 100 ワットの蛍光灯　　　　　　　　　100-watt fluorescent light

電池

- □ 単一電池　　　size D battery
- □ 単二電池　　　size C battery
- □ 単三電池　　　AA battery　　　＊ double A と読みます。
- □ 単四電池　　　AAA battery　　＊ triple A と読みます。
- □ 充電式電池　　charging battery
- □ 充電時間　　　charging time
- □ 電池の寿命　　battery life

家電製品

- □ A 46-inch flat screen HDTV, LCD TV. Full manufacturer's warranty.
  ［46インチ、薄型ハイビジョンテレビ、液晶テレビ。メーカー完全保証］
    * HDTV = High-definition television
    * LCD = Liquid crystal display
- □ A plasma display panel (PDP) is a type of flat panel display common to large TV displays (32 inches or larger).
  ［プラズマディスプレイパネル（PDP）は、（32インチ以上の）大型ディスプレイに広く使われる薄型パネルである］
- □ A full-size refrigerator. Choose between 18 and 21 cu. ft.
  ［普通サイズの冷蔵庫。容積18〜21立方フィートの間で選択可］
    * cu. ft. = cubic feet
- □ Tumble Dryer — Capacity: 5.99 kg, Power Source: Electric
  ［タンブラー乾燥機—容量：5.99キログラム、動力源：電気］
- □ Most standard-size dishwashers use about 2.4 gallons of water to wash a load of dishes.
  ［ほとんどの標準サイズの食器洗い機は、1回の洗浄に約2.4ガロンの水を必要とする］

カメラ、写真

カメラ、レンズ

- Shutter speed: 1/250. Focal length: 9.1875 mm.
  [シャッタースピード：250 分の 1、焦点距離：9.1875 ミリメートル]
- The camera has an aperture range of F1.8 to F16.
  [このカメラの絞りは、F1.8 から F16 までである]
- I bought the 50 mm f / 1.2 lens.
  [私は、50 ミリメートルの f / 1.2 のレンズを購入した]
    * F / f は focus（ピント、焦点）の f です。数字が大きくなるほど、aperture（絞り）が狭くなります。

〈その他〉

- デジタル一眼レフカメラ　　　　　digital single-lens reflex camera
- 300 ミリメートル、f 2.8 の望遠レンズ　　300 mm f 2.8 telephoto lens
- 120 度の広角レンズ　　　　　　　120° wide-angle lens
- 1500 万画素　　　　15,000,000 pixels = 15 megapixels / 15 MP
    * pixel = pictures → pix（picture の複数形の省略形）+ element（要素）
- 連続撮影速度―毎秒 3 コマ　　　　　　　　　　　　　3 pps/fps
    * pps = pictures per second、fps = frames per second

フィルム

- メモリーカード　　　memory card
- 24 枚撮りフィルム　　24-exposure film

焼き増し、枚数、引き伸ばし

- Permission to reprint photo: Less than 2,000 copies, $80.
  [写真焼き増し許可料金：2,000 枚以下 80 ドル]
- Scan a photo and enlarge it to print at 8 × 10 on an inkjet.
  [写真をスキャンして、インクジェットで印刷し、8 インチ× 10 インチに引き伸ばす]

その他（家族、選挙、法律）　Miscellaneous (Family、Election、Law)

家　族

～人家族

- We are a family of four. / There are four of us in my family.
  ［うちは 4 人家族だ］

～世、～代目、～世代

- She is a second-generation Japanese-American.
  ［彼女は、日系アメリカ人 2 世だ］
- Henry VIII had six wives.　　　（the eighth）
  ［ヘンリー 8 世には、6 人の妻がいた］
- I am the fourth generation involved in the family business.
  ［私が家業の 4 代目だ］
- Five generations of his family have gone to the same village school.
  ［彼の家族は、5 世代にわたって同じ村の学校に通っている］

～親等

- A first-degree relative is a parent or offspring; a second-degree relative is a sibling, grandparent or grandchild.
  ［一親等は両親、子どもを指し、二親等は兄弟/姉妹、祖父母、孫を指す］

その他

□ 育ての親、里親	foster parent
□ 養子	foster child、adopted child
□ 連れ子	stepchild
□ 異父姉妹、異母姉妹	half sister
□ 異父兄弟、異母兄弟	half brother

選挙

票、議席

- The proposal passed by a large margin, with a vote of 45 in favor, 2 against, and 3 abstaining.
  [その法案は、賛成45票、反対2票、棄権3票の大差で可決された]
- They won 196 seats in the general election.
  [彼らは、総選挙で196議席獲得した]

任期

- Councilors are usually elected for a term of four years.
  [議員は、通常、4年の任期で選出される]
- He is battling for a third term in the mayoral elections on 1 May.
  [彼は、5月1日におこなわれる市長選で、3選を目指して戦っている]

法律

条項

- In Article 9, Japan promises never again to go to war against other nations.
  [第9条で、日本は戦争放棄を約束している]
  ＊条項はその他、section、clause なども使います。

処分、罰金、判決

- The company suspended him from duty for 3 months.
  [会社は彼を、3ヵ月の停職処分にした]
- He will have to face either a year's jail sentence or a $20,000 fine.
  [彼は1年の実刑判決か、2万ドルの罰金刑のどちらかを受けなければならないだろう]

- [ ] He was sentenced to one year's imprisonment with three years' probation.
    ［彼は懲役1年、執行猶予3年の判決を受けた］
- [ ] The judge said that the defendant must serve at least 20 years.
    ［被告は、少なくとも20年は刑に服すべきだと裁判官は言った］
- [ ] He spent more than 11 years behind bars for his crimes.
    ［彼は、罪を犯して11年間以上、刑務所に入っていた］
- [ ] He was appealing his conviction and was set free on bail of 500 million yen.
    ［彼は、有罪判決に対して上告して、5億円の保釈金で釈放された］

19 電気器具 / 設備、カメラ、写真、その他 (家族、選挙、法律) ・徹底トレーニング

1 CDから流れてくる英文を聴き、カッコの部分を書き取ってください。

1) Under a new Federal law, you have the right to receive a free copy of your credit report (   ) every (   ) months from each of the (   ) nationwide consumer reporting companies.

2) If the dryer is (   ) volts and (   ) amps, you can use only (   ) amp wire {(   ) gauge minimum} and a double-pole (   ) amp breaker.

3) There were (   ) foster children in the city in March (   ), a (   ) percent decrease from the (   ) children living in foster care in March (   ).

4) A man linked to the seizure of nearly £(   ) worth of cocaine has been jailed for more than (   ) years.

5) The offence carries a fine of up to €(   ) {£(   )} or a maximum prison sentence of (   ) year.

6) Shutter speed: (   ) sec. Aperture: (   ). Exposure mode: Av ISO: (   ).

7) (   ) generations of young people — aged (   ), (   ) and (   ) — were interviewed.

8) The Labour Party won (   ) seats in the (   ) election. In (   ) the Labour Party won (   ) seats, and in (   ) the Conservatives won (   ) seats, Labour (   ) and the Liberals (   ).

9) I went to a friend's house and was able to enlarge an (   ) photo to a (   ) poster using (   ) sheets of paper.

10) He won ( ) votes out of ( ), far more than the ( ) votes that would have guaranteed him victory, leaving his ( ) rivals trailing far behind.

解答

1) Under a new Federal law, you have the right to receive a free copy of your credit report (once) every (12) months from each of the (three) nationwide consumer reporting companies.
   〔新たな連邦法のもとでは、貴殿は 12 ヵ月ごとに全国消費者報告会社 3 社から、無料の信用報告書を受け取る権利があります〕

2) If the dryer is (220) volts and (30) amps, you can use only (30) amp wire {(10) gauge minimum} and a double-pole (30) amp breaker.
   〔乾燥機が、220 ボルト 30 アンペアの場合、30 アンペアワイヤー（最低 10 ゲージ規格）と 2 極 30 アンペアブレーカーのみ使用できる〕

3) There were (16,982) foster children in the city in March (2008), a (40) percent decrease from the (27,981) children living in foster care in March (2002).
   〔2008 年 3 月時点で、都市には 16,982 人の養子がいた。2002 年 3 月の養子 27,981 人と比較すると、40％の減少になる〕

4) A man linked to the seizure of nearly £(24,000) worth of cocaine has been jailed for more than (two) years.
   〔24,000 ポンド相当の、コカイン押収に関連のある男は、2 年以上投獄されている〕

5) The offence carries a fine of up to €(25,000) {£(17,400)} or a maximum prison sentence of (one) year.
   〔その犯罪は、25,000 ユーロ（17,400 ポンド）までの罰金刑か、最高 1 年の実刑である〕

6) Shutter speed: (1/1,000) sec. Aperture: (2.0). Exposure mode: Av. ISO: (100).
   〔シャッタースピード：1/1,000 秒、絞り：2.0、露光モード：Av. ISO：100〕

7) (Three) generations of young people — aged (11-12), (16-18) and (24-25)— were interviewed.
　　［3世代にわたる若者―11〜12歳、16〜18歳、そして24〜25歳がインタビューされた］

8) The Labour Party won (63) seats in the (1918) election. In (1922) the Labour Party won (142) seats, and in (1924) the Conservatives won (258) seats, Labour (191) and the Liberals (158).
　　［労働党は、1918年の選挙で63議席獲得。1922年では、労働党は142議席獲得。1924年には、保守党は258議席、労働党は191議席、そして自由党は158議席だった］
　　　　labour（英）= labor（米）
　　＊ここでのthe Labour Partyは、イギリスの労働党を指しています。

9) I went to a friend's house and was able to enlarge an (8 × 10) photo to a (3 × 3) poster using (9) sheets of paper.
　　［私は友人の家へ行き、9枚のシートを使って、8×10の写真を3×3のポスターに引き伸ばすことができた］

10) He won (481) votes out of (702), far more than the (352) votes that would have guaranteed him victory, leaving his (two) rivals trailing far behind.
　　［彼は、702票中481票を獲得した。それは、勝利ラインの352票をはるかに上回り、2人のライバルに大きく水をあけた］

7 教育、文化、スポーツ
Education、Culture、Sports

学校、映画、演劇、音楽、スポーツ

学校

学年

- □ 小学1年生　　in (the) first grade、first-grader
- □ 中学3年生　　in (the) 9th grade
- □ 高校1年生　　in (the) 10th grade
- □ 高校2年生　　high school junior、in (the) 11th grade
- □ 高校3年生　　high school senior、in (the) 12th grade
- □ 大学1年生　　freshman
- □ 大学2年生　　sophomore
- □ 大学3年生　　junior
- □ 大学4年生　　senior

学期

- □ 1学期　　　　first term
- □ 前期/後期　　first semester / second semester

映画、演劇

上映時間、観客動員数など

- □ 映画は上映時間2時間だ。　　The movie has a 2-hour screen time.
　　　　　　　　　　　　　　　The running time for the film is 2 hours.
- □ 観客動員数70万人　　　　　It has been seen by 700,000 people.
- □ 興業売上げ10億ドル　　　　one-billion-dollars in box-office revenue
- □ 初演　　　　　　　　　　　premiere

☐ 5ヵ月の興行	5-month run
☐ 3幕2場10行目	Act III, Scene ii, line 10
	（Act three, Scene two, line ten）

音　楽

曲

☐ 12曲入りCD	CD with 12 tracks、12-track CD
☐ モーツァルト3曲	three pieces by Mozart
☐ 交響曲40番	Symphony No. 40

拍　子

☐ 2拍子	double time
☐ 3拍子	triple time
☐ 4拍子	quadruple time
☐ 4分の3拍子	three-quarter time

スポーツ

野　球

☐ 5回の表/裏に	in the top / bottom of the fifth inning
☐ 3点を加えた	added three runs
☐ 2点取られた	gave up two runs
☐ カウントワンスリー	The count is three balls, one strike、three one
☐ 四球	a walk、base on balls
☐ 二塁打	two-base hit
☐ 打率3割2分5厘	batting average of .325 （three twenty-five）
☐ 5打数2安打	2-5　　　　　　　（two for five）
☐ 防御率2.28	2.28 ERA　　　　（earned run average）
☐ 7回戦（勝負）	best-of-seven series
☐ 7試合中4試合に勝った	won four out of seven games
☐ 背番号55	player number 55

ゴルフ

☐ 5番ホール	the fifth (hole)
☐ パー3ホール	Par 3
☐ ハンデ28	handicap of 28
☐ 3連続バーディ	three consecutive birdies
☐ ホールインワン	hole in one、an ace
☐ 3打	three strokes
☐ フォーサム	foursome

サッカー

☐ 前半	the first half
☐ 後半	the second half
☐ 3分間のロスタイム	3-minute injury time
☐ 2点リード	two goals up / ahead、leading by two goals

テニス

☐ 30-30	thirty all
☐ 0-15	love fifteen
☐ 1回戦	first round
☐ 第3セット	the third set

その他

☐ 10勝2敗	record of 10 wins and 2 defeats、10 wins and 2 losses、10-2 record（ten to two）
☐ 3対3の引き分け	3-3 tie（three to three）
☐ 0対0の引き分け	no score draw
☐ 7連勝/連覇	7-game winning streak、seven straight wins
☐ 世界ランキング5位	rank 5th in the world、5th in the world ranking
☐ 記録を1秒更新する	break / smash the record by one second

20 教育、文化、スポーツ・徹底トレーニング

1 CDから流れてくる英文を聴き、カッコの部分を書き取ってください。

1) The Americans finished (　　) in total medals with (　　). China finished with (　　), (　　) more than it won (　　) years ago.

2) Her (　　), (　　) victory gave her a (　　) Wimbledon singles title.

3) A panel of judges considered more than (　　) works for best drama and recommended (　　) finalists to the board.

4) He clocked in at (　　) in his (　　) major marathon, with a fellow Kenyan runner (　　) at (　　).

5) She won (　　), (　　), (　　) to extend a streak that has lasted (　　) years.

6) He has written just (　　) plays in (　　) years.

7) The singer and her band have spent more than (　　) hours rehearsing for the (　　) show which is broken into (　　) sets.

8) Saturday's baseball game was halted in the top of the (　　) inning with the score tied (　　).

9) The (　　)-year-old Beijing double-gold medalist won the S (　　) (　　) m freestyle, smashing the old record by (　　) seconds.

10) She finally fell to the Portuguese judo world champion in the (　　) kg category, on a (　　) refereeing flag decision.

136

解 答

1) The Americans finished (first) in total medals with (110). China finished with (100), (36) more than it won (four) years ago.
   [米国が、全110個のメダルを獲得して1位となった。中国は4年前より36個増の100個を獲得した]

2) Her (7-5), (6-4) victory gave her a (fifth) Wimbledon singles title.
   [彼女は、7対5、6対4で勝利し、5度目のウィンブルドンシングルスのタイトルを手にした]

3) A panel of judges considered more than (150) works for best drama and recommended (three) finalists to the board.
   [審査員団は、150を超す作品の中から熟慮の末、最優秀ドラマとして3作の最終候補を選考委員会に推薦した]

4) He clocked in at (2:07:37) in his (first) major marathon, with a fellow Kenyan runner (third) at (2:11:39).
   [彼は、初めての大きなマラソン大会で、2時間7分37秒を記録、同じくケニヤ人のランナーが、2時間11分39秒で3位に入った]

5) She won (6-2), (4-6), (7-6) to extend a streak that has lasted (5 1/2) years.
   [彼女は、6-2、4-6、7-6で勝ち、5年半続く連勝記録を伸ばした]

6) He has written just (five) plays in (18) years.
   [彼は18年間で、ちょうど5つの戯曲を書いたことになる]

7) The singer and her band have spent more than (650) hours rehearsing for the (two-hour) show which is broken into (four) sets.
   [その歌手と彼女のバンドは、4部構成の2時間のショーの本番に向けて、650時間以上をリハーサルに費やしてきた]

8) Saturday's baseball game was halted in the top of the (eighth) inning with the score tied (3-3).
   [土曜日の野球の試合は、8回の表、3対3の引き分けで中断された]

9) The (17)-year-old Beijing double-gold medalist won the S (6) (100) m freestyle, smashing the old record by (1.3) seconds.
   [北京オリンピックで、2つの金メダルを獲った17歳の選手が、S6クラス、100メートル自由形で勝ち、記録を1.3秒更新した]

10)　She finally fell to the Portuguese judo world champion in the (52) kg category, on a (3-0) refereeing flag decision.
　　　［彼女は柔道 52 キログラム級で、ポルトガルの世界チャンピオンに、3 対 0 の判定で結局負けてしまった］

衣料品、靴、指輪サイズ一覧　Clothing, Shoes, Rings

衣料品

衣料品のサイズ表記は、国、メーカーによってばらばらで、換算も違うことが多いので注意が必要です。以下は、あくまでも目安になります。

女性用衣料品サイズ

〈洋服〉

日	7	9	11	13	15	17
米	8	10	12	14	16	18
英	32	34	36	38	40	42
欧	36	38	40	42	44	46

＊通常、日本の7～9号が米・英・欧州のSサイズ、11～13号がMサイズ、15～17号がLサイズに相当します。

〈ボトム―ウエストサイズ〉

cm	56	58	61	63	66	68
inch	26	27	28	29	30	31

男性用衣料品サイズ

〈スーツ、コート〉

日	S		M		L		XL	
米・英	34	36	38	40	42	44	46	48
欧	44	46	48	50	52	54	56	58

〈ワイシャツ〉

日	36	37	38	39	40	41	42	43
米・英	14	14 1/2	15	15 1/2	16	16 1/2	17	17 1/2
欧	36	37	38	39	40	41	42	43

〈ボトム―ウエストサイズ〉

cm	73	76	78	81	83	86
inch	29	30	31	32	33	34

帽子

日 (cm)	53	54	55	56	57	58	59	60
米・英	6 5/8	6 3/4	6 7/8	7	7 1/8	7 1/4	7 3/8	7 1/2
欧 (inch)	20 3/4	21 1/8	21 1/2	21 7/8	22 1/4	22 5/8	23	23 1/2

＊通常、日本の53〜55センチメートルが米・英・欧州のSサイズ、56〜57センチメートルがMサイズ、58〜59センチメートルがLサイズ、60〜61センチメートルがXLサイズに相当します。

靴

靴のサイズ表記も、国・メーカーによってばらばらで、換算も違うことが多いので注意が必要です。以下は、あくまでも目安になります。

女性用靴サイズ

日	22	22.5	23	23.5	24	24.5	25
米	5	5 1/2	6	6 1/2	7	7 1/2	8
英	3 1/2	4	4 1/2	5	5 1/2	6	6 1/2
欧	35	36	37	38	38	39	39

＊1/2の読み方は、halfです。

男性用靴サイズ

日	24.5	25	25.5	26	26.5	27	27.5
米	6 1/2	7	7 1/2	8	8 1/2	9	9 1/2
英	6	6 1/2	7	7 1/2	8	8 1/2	9
欧	40	40 1/2	41	41 1/2	42	42 1/2	43

指　輪

指輪サイズ

日	9	10	11	12	13	14	15	16	17
米	5	5 1/2	6	6 1/2	6 1/2-7	7-7 1/2	7 1/2-8	8	8 1/2
英	J	K	L	L-M	M-N	N-O	O-P	P	Q
欧	49	50	51	52	53	54	55	56	57

8 単位
Units

長さ、幅 Length、Width

長さ

ミリメートル

- The metal was 13 mm long.
    [その金属は、長さ 13 ミリメートルだった]
- Shaft length: 57.0 mm
    [柄の長さ：57.0 ミリメートル]

センチメートル

- The magnetic alloy rods are 1.4 cm long.
    [磁性合金ロッドは、長さ 1.4 センチメートルだ]
- The leaves of the plant can reach a maximum length of about 28 cm.
    [その植物の葉は、最大約 28 センチメートルの長さにまでなる]

メートル

- It is an 800-meter-long embankment of rock and sand.
    [それは、岩と砂でできた長さ 800 メートルの堤防だ]
- The dam is 175 m in length.
    [そのダムは、長さ 175 メートルである]

キロメートル

- The enemy's supply lines are more than 500 km long.
    [敵の補給ラインは、500 キロメートル以上の長さである]

□ The island has a length of 8 km from west to east.
　［その島は、西から東まで 8 キロメートルの長さだ］

インチ

□ The surgical scissors are 6.6 inches long.
　［外科手術用のハサミは、6.6 インチの長さだ］
　　＊ 1 inch ＝ 2.54 cm

フィート

□ The fortress walls of reddish stones are 1,500 feet long.
　［赤みを帯びた石造りのその要塞の壁は、1,500 フィートの長さだ］
　　＊ 1 foot ＝ 12 inches ＝ 30.48 cm

ヤード

□ The bridge was about 100 yards long and had a brick bottom.
　［その橋は、約 100 ヤードの長さで、底面はれんが造りだった］
　　＊ 1 yard ＝ 3 feet ＝ 36 inches ＝ 0.9144 m

マイル

□ The 90-mile-long Suez Canal was built with French engineering and Egyptian labor.
　［長さ 90 マイルのスエズ運河は、フランスの技術とエジプト人の労働力を使って建設された］
　　＊ 1 mile ＝ 1,760 yards ＝ 1,609.344 m ≒ 1.6 km

幅

ミリメートル

□ The smallest possible broadcast quality camera has a lens 10 mm wide.
　［可能な限り小さい、放送品質カメラのレンズの幅は、10 ミリメートルだ］

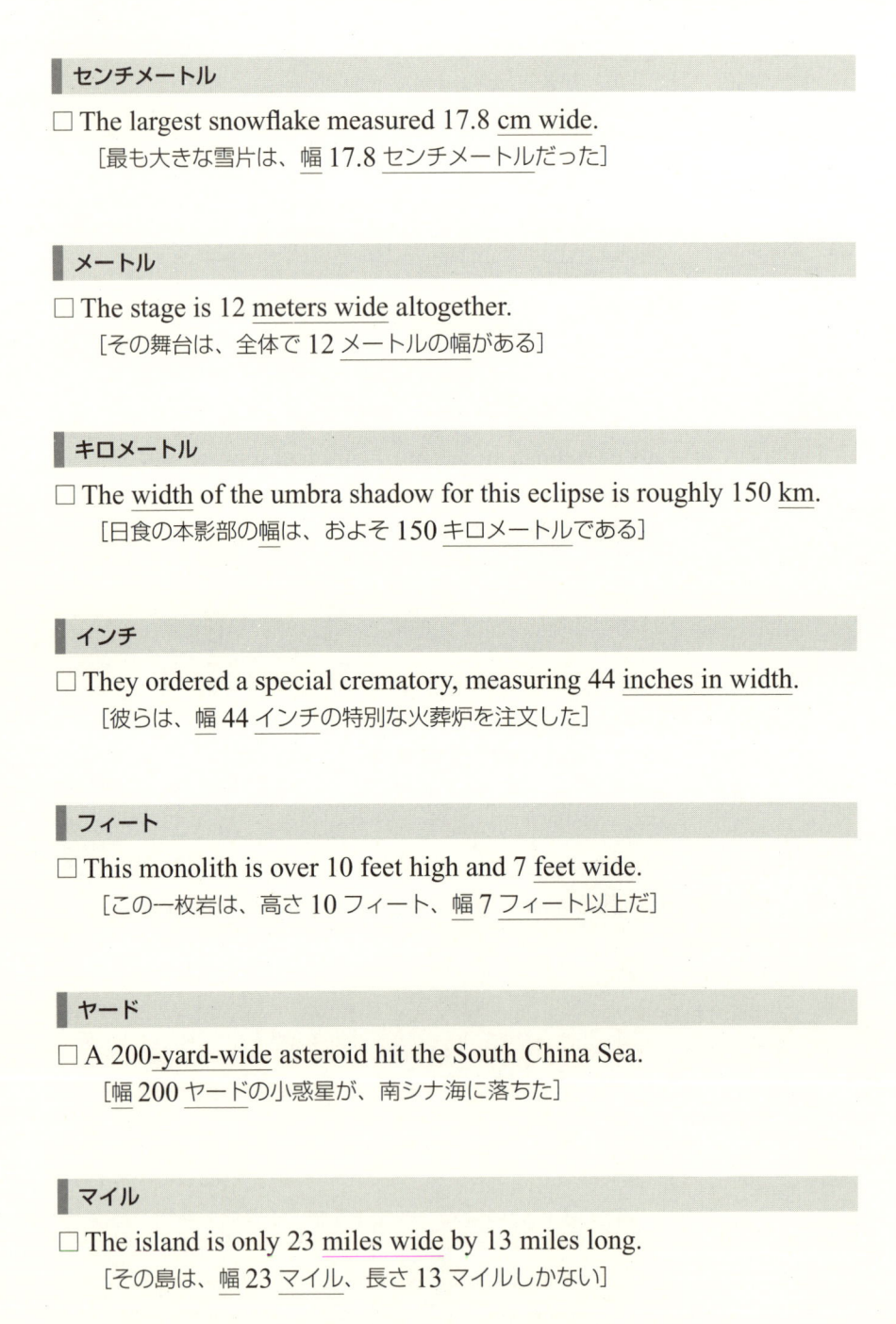

センチメートル

☐ The largest snowflake measured 17.8 cm wide.
　[最も大きな雪片は、幅 17.8 センチメートルだった]

メートル

☐ The stage is 12 meters wide altogether.
　[その舞台は、全体で 12 メートルの幅がある]

キロメートル

☐ The width of the umbra shadow for this eclipse is roughly 150 km.
　[日食の本影部の幅は、およそ 150 キロメートルである]

インチ

☐ They ordered a special crematory, measuring 44 inches in width.
　[彼らは、幅 44 インチの特別な火葬炉を注文した]

フィート

☐ This monolith is over 10 feet high and 7 feet wide.
　[この一枚岩は、高さ 10 フィート、幅 7 フィート以上だ]

ヤード

☐ A 200-yard-wide asteroid hit the South China Sea.
　[幅 200 ヤードの小惑星が、南シナ海に落ちた]

マイル

☐ The island is only 23 miles wide by 13 miles long.
　[その島は、幅 23 マイル、長さ 13 マイルしかない]

その他

半径

- Homes within a 218-yard radius of the property had to be evacuated.
  [その土地の半径 218 ヤード以内にある世帯は、避難しなければならなかった]
- We drew a circle with a radius of 32 meters on the school field.
  [私たちは、校庭に半径 32 メートルの円を描いた]

直径

- The dome is 22 feet in diameter.
  [そのドームは、直径 22 フィートである]
- The telescope has a 60-millimeter-diameter primary mirror.
  [その望遠鏡の主鏡は、直径 60 ミリメートルである]

口径、内径

- He was carrying a gold-plated .38-caliber pistol.
  [彼は、金めっきが施された 38 口径のピストルを所持していた]
    * .38-caliber ＝ .38 cal. ＝ 0.38 インチの口径
    * 整数の 0 は省略して書きます。読み方は、小数点以下を基数で読みます。例文の「.38-caliber pistol」は、thirty-eight / point thirty-eight caliber pistol になります。

周囲、円周

- The lake measures about 1.3 miles in circumference and is used by some local schools for hiking.
  [その周囲約 1.3 マイルの湖は、地元の学校がハイキングに利用している]

☐ Mercury has a circumference of about 15,300 km.
　［水星は、円周約 1 万 5,300 キロメートルである］

21 長さ、幅・徹底トレーニング Step 1

1 CDから流れてくる英文を聴き、カッコの部分を書き取ってください。

1) The cluster bombs are (   ) cm in diameter and (   ) cm in length and they are cylindrical in shape.

2) The monument walls are nearly (   ) miles {(   ) km} long.

3) Authorities have evacuated buildings within a (   )-mile radius around the site, including (   ) schools and (   ) retirement home.

4) The boats were (   ) feet long, (   ) feet (   ) inches wide, and carried (   ) tons of cargo when fully laden.

5) The (   )-mile {(   )-kilometer}-long path runs over the farmer's field.

6) The box is (   ) m long, over (   ) m wide and (   ) m high.

7) The modern house was (   ) feet by (   ) feet and (   ) stories high.

8) In total, the figure is (   ) km {(   ) miles} long and (   ) km {(   ) miles} wide.

9) There are (   ) landfill sites within a (   )-kilometer radius.

10) The main structure is a (   )-kilometer {(   )-mile}-circumference accelerator ring of superconducting magnets.

> 解 答

1) The cluster bombs are (6) cm in diameter and (16) cm in length and they are cylindrical in shape.
   [そのクラスター爆弾は、直径6センチメートル、長さ16センチメートルで円筒形をしている]

2) The monument walls are nearly (1.5) miles {(2.4) km} long.
   [その記念碑の壁は、およそ1.5マイル（2.4キロメートル）の長さだ]

3) Authorities have evacuated buildings within a (150)-mile radius around the site, including (two) schools and (one) retirement home.
   [当局は、現場から半経150マイル以内の建物を、避難のため明け渡させた。それには学校2校と、老人ホーム1施設が含まれている]

4) The boats were (65) feet long, (7) feet (6) inches wide, and carried (22) tons of cargo when fully laden.
   [それらのボートは、長さ65フィート、幅7フィート6インチ、そして22トンの貨物を積載できた]

5) The (135)-mile {(217)-kilometer}-long path runs over the farmer's field.
   [農場には、長さ135マイル（217キロメートル）の散歩道が続いている]

6) The box is (240) m long, over (100) m wide and (50) m high.
   [その貯蔵庫のサイズは、長さ240メートル、幅100メートル以上、高さ50メートルである]

7) The modern house was (37) feet by (25) feet and (3) stories high.
   [そのモダンな家は、37フィート×25フィートの大きさで、3階建てだった]

8) In total, the figure is (2.5) km {(1.6) miles} long and (2.2) km {(1.4) miles} wide.
   [全体でその像は、長さ2.5キロメートル（1.6マイル）、幅2.2キロメートル（1.4マイル）の大きさだ]

9) There are (five) landfill sites within a (two)-kilometer radius.
   [半径2キロメートル以内に、5つの埋め立て処分地がある]

10) The main structure is a (27)-kilometer {(17)-mile}-circumference accelerator ring of superconducting magnets.
    [主要構造は、円周27キロメートル（17マイル）の超電導磁石環状加速器である]

2 2TRACK 2

CDから流れてくる日本語を聴き、即座に英語に直して発話してください。（＊日本語の後ポーズがあって、その後すぐに英語が流れます）

1)
2)
3)
4)
5)

解 答

1) 長さ37センチメートル　　　37 cm long
2) 幅6フィート2インチ　　　　6 feet 2 inches wide
3) 長さ45ミリメートル　　　　45 mm in length
4) 幅3〜5キロメートル　　　　a width of 3-5 km
5) 半径50マイル　　　　　　　a 50-mile radius

3 以下の日本語を英語に直して発話してください。 2TRACK 3

1) 幅50ヤードの彗星

2) そのダムは長さ175メートルである。

3) 長さ18インチのポール

4) 長さ約8センチメートルの紙飛行機

5) 幅約23キロメートル

解 答

1) a 50-yard-wide comet
2) The dam is 175 m in length.
3) an 18-inch pole
4) paper planes about 8 cm long
5) a width of about 23 km

8 単位

体重、身長 / 体長　Weight、Height / Length

体重

グラム

☐ Premature babies who weigh more than 500 grams have a 40 to 50% chance of survival.
　［体重 500 グラム以上の未熟児は、40〜50％の生存率である］
☐ The male and female cubs weighed in at 600 grams and 400 grams respectively.
　［オスとメスのトラの赤ちゃんの体重は、それぞれ 600 グラムと 400 グラムだった］

キログラム

☐ She weighs 48 kg.
　［彼女の体重は 48 キログラムだ］
☐ Leopard seals can weigh up to 500 kg.
　［ヒョウアザラシは、重さ 500 キログラムにもなる］

ポンド

☐ She lost 15 pounds during her journey in 2008.
　［彼女は 2008 年の旅行中に、15 ポンド体重が減った］
☐ Bears can weigh up to 1,716 pounds and have large appetites to satisfy.
　［熊は体重が 1,716 ポンドにまでなり、旺盛な食欲を持つ］
　　＊ 1 pound ≒ 454 g

ストーン

☐ Somebody of my height and build (I'm 172 cm) should weigh between 10 stone 7 and 11 stone 7.
　［私と同じくらいの身長と体型（172 センチメートル）の人は、体重 10.7〜11.7 ストーンであるべきだ］

150

* 1 stone = 14 pounds ≒ 6.35 kg
* stone は、重量の単位で、通常、人間の体重を表すときに使われます。そして現在はイギリスのみで使用されています。

身長 / 体長

ミリメートル

☐ The bat is less than 50 mm long, weighing less than 9 grams.
［そのコウモリは、体長 50 ミリメートル以下で、体重 9 グラム以下だ］

センチメートル

☐ I'm 159.5 cm tall. / I'm 159.5 cm. / I'm 159.5.
［私の身長は、159.5 センチメートルだ］

メートル

☐ He is 1.6 meters tall and weighs about 50 kg.
［彼は身長 1.6 メートルで、体重約 50 キログラムだ］

☐ The biggest Bluefin tuna weighs up to 700 kg and can measure over 3 meters in length.
［最も大きなクロマグロは、重さ 700 キログラムまでになり、体長は 3 メートルを超える］

フィート（フット）、インチ

☐ He is 6 feet 2 inches tall. / He is six foot two. / He is six-two. / He is 6'2".
［彼の身長は、6 フィート 2 インチだ］
　　* 1 foot = 12 inches = 30.48cm　　* 1 inch = 2.54 cm
　　*「'」（＝プライム記号）と「"」（＝ダブルプライム記号）は、それぞれ、フィートとインチの単位記号です。

22 体重、身長 / 体長・徹底トレーニング Step 1

1 CD から流れてくる英文を聴き、カッコの部分を書き取ってください。

1) Police described both the men as white, about (　) feet (　) inches {(　) cm} tall and of slim build.

2) The bear was (　) months old and had grown to (　) kg {(　) pounds}.

3) At the age of (　), he now weighs (　) kg and is (　) cm tall.

4) I lost (　) pounds and (　) dress sizes.

5) She was (　) cm {(　) feet (　) inches} tall and weighed (　) kg {(　) pounds}.

解答

1) Police described both the men as white, about (5) feet (9) inches {(180) cm} tall and of slim build.
   [警察は2人の男について、両者とも白人で、身長約5フィート9インチ（180センチメートル）、やせ型だと述べた]

2) The bear was (six) months old and had grown to (28) kg {(62) pounds}.
   [その熊は生後6ヵ月で、28キログラム（62ポンド）だった]

3) At the age of (72), he now weighs (88) kg and is (187) cm tall.
   [年齢は72歳で、彼は現在、体重88キログラム、身長187センチメートルだ]

4) I lost (20) pounds and (2) dress sizes.
   [私は20ポンド減量し、洋服のサイズが2つ小さくなった]

5) She was (169) cm {(5) feet (7) inches} tall and weighed (50) kg {(110) pounds}.
   [彼女は身長169センチメートル（5フィート7インチ）で、体重50キログラム（110ポンド）だった]

2 CDから流れてくる日本語を聴き、即座に英語に直して発話してください。(＊日本語の後ポーズがあって、その後すぐに英語が流れます)　 2TRACK 5

8 単位

1)
2)
3)

解　答
1)　78 ポンド　　　　　　　　78 pounds
2)　14 インチ　　　　　　　　14 inches
3)　90 キログラム　　　　　　90 kg

3 以下の日本語を英語に直して発話してください。　 2TRACK 6

1)　私は身長 173 センチメートルだ。

2)　彼は体重 62 キログラムだ。

3)　彼らの猫は体重 5 ポンドだ。

解　答
1)　I am 173 cm tall.
2)　He weighs 62 kg.
3)　Their cat weighs 5 pounds.

重さ　Weight

ミリグラム

☐ The panel set a 2,000-milligram daily upper limit for vitamin C from a combination of food and supplements.
　［委員会は、食物とサプリメントの組み合わせから摂取するビタミンCの上限を、1日2,000ミリグラムに設定した］

グラム

☐ He pleaded guilty to possession of more than 100 grams of heroin.
　［彼は、100グラム以上のヘロイン所持の罪状を認めた］

キログラム

☐ Melamine levels considered safe are 1 milligram per kilogram of infant formula.
　［安全だと考えられるメラミンレベルは、乳児用ミルク1キログラムあたり1ミリグラムだ］

ポンド

☐ They earn about 18 cents per pound.
　［彼らは1ポンドにつき、約18セントを得る］
☐ The bomb contained more than 1,100 lb of explosives.
　［その爆弾には、1,100ポンド以上の火薬が詰められていた］
　　＊ lb = libra（ラテン語）　重さの単位、ポンドを表す記号。ポンドと読みます。
　　＊ 1 pound = 16 ounces ≒ 454 g

トン

☐ The factory produces 42,000 tons of sugar a year.
　　［その工場は、1年に4万2,000トンの砂糖を生産する］
　　　＊ ton(s) は、tonne(s) ともつづります。
　　　＊ 1 ton ＝ 1,000 kg

オンス

☐ Gold prices climbed past $900 an ounce.
　　［金の値段が上昇して、1オンスあたり900ドルを超えた］
　　　＊ 1 ounce ＝ 1/16 pound ≒ 28g

23　重さ・徹底トレーニング Step 1

1　CD から流れてくる英文を聴き、カッコの部分を書き取ってください。

1) (　　) months ago, nearly (　　) tonnes of cannabis were seized, and in March (　　) men were arrested transporting (　　) tonnes of the drug.

2) (　　) pound of fat includes the energy equivalent of (　　) calories.

3) Overall (　　) milligrams of liquid methadone and (　　) methadone tablets were taken.

4) A (　　) oz. jar with (　　) proven ingredients. The most advanced hair growth topical gel in the world. Based on (　　) years of research.

5) The government recommends salt consumption of no more than (　　) grams per day {(　　) g or less for children}, but most adults consume around (　　) g.

解答

1) (Two) months ago, nearly (eight) tonnes of cannabis were seized and in March (six) men were arrested transporting (ten) tonnes of the drug.
   [2ヵ月前、8トン近い大麻が押収された。そして3月には、6人の男が10トンの薬物を密輸して逮捕された]

2) (One) pound of fat includes the energy equivalent of (3,500) calories.
   [1ポンドの脂肪は、3,500カロリーに相当するエネルギーを含む]

3) Overall (420) milligrams of liquid methadone and (12) methadone tablets were taken.
   [全部で420ミリグラムの液剤メタドンと、12個のメタドンの錠剤が摂取された]

4) A (2) oz. jar with (12) proven ingredients. The most advanced hair growth topical gel in the world. Based on (20) years of research.
   ［2 オンス瓶。実証済み 12 成分含有。世界で最も進化した話題の増毛ジェル。20 年の研究に基づく］

5) The government recommends salt consumption of no more than (6) grams per day ｛(3) g or less for children｝, but most adults consume around (12) g.
   ［政府は、塩分摂取を 1 日わずか 6 グラム（子どもは 3 グラム以下）にするよう推奨しているが、ほとんどの大人が 12 グラム程度を摂取している］

8 単位

🎧 2TRACK 8

2 CD から流れてくる日本語を聴き、即座に英語に直して発話してください。（＊日本語の後ポーズがあって、その後すぐに英語が流れます）

1)　　　　　　　　　　　2)
3)

解　答

1)	7.9 ミリグラム	7.9 milligrams
2)	65 ポンド	65 pounds
3)	30 キログラム	30 kg

3 以下の日本語を英語に直して発話してください。　🎧 2TRACK 9

1) 1 キロあたり 2.5 ミリグラム

2) 一晩に約 200 グラム

3) 100 ポンドの戦時中の爆弾

解　答

1) 2.5 milligrams per kilogram
2) around 200 grams in one night
3) a 100-pound wartime bomb

深さ / 奥行き、厚さ　Depth、Thickness

深さ / 奥行き

ミリメートル

☐ The soil thermometer is showing the temperature to be around 4°C at 100 mm deep.
　［地中温度計は、深さ 100 ミリメートルで摂氏約 4 度を示している］

センチメートル

☐ The boxes are grey plastic, 40 cm long by 20 cm wide and 12 cm deep.
　［箱はグレーのプラスチック製で、長さ 40 センチメートル、幅 20 センチメートル、奥行き 12 センチメートルだ］

☐ The snow is very thick with a depth of about 80 cm.
　［雪はとても厚く積もり、約 80 センチメートルの深さである］

メートル

☐ The soil was dug up to a depth of half a meter.
　［地面は 0.5 メートルの深さまで掘られていた］

キロメートル

☐ Silt sediments are thought to be 10 km deep.
　［沈泥の沈殿物は、10 キロメートルの深さと考えられている］

インチ

☐ The whole garden was flooded to a depth of six inches.
　［庭全体が、6 インチの深さまで水浸しになった］

単位

フィート

□ The crater was 20 feet deep.
　[そのクレーターは 20 フィートの深さだった]
□ Business was at a standstill with three-foot-deep snow on some of the streets.
　[積雪が 3 フィートの深さに達した通りもあり、商売がストップした]
　　* 1 foot = 30.48 cm
　　* foot の複数形は feet ですが、five-foot-deep のようにハイフンでつなぐ場合は形容詞となるので、単数の foot を使います。

ヤード

□ The mine's depth was only 100 yards.
　[鉱坑の深さは、わずか 100 ヤードだった]

マイル

□ The epicenter was 93 miles deep.
　[震源の深さは、93 マイルだった]
　　* 1 mile = 1,760 yards = 1,609.344 m ≒ 1.6 km

厚さ

ミリメートル

□ The costume is made out of two-millimeter-thick felt.
　[その衣装は、厚さ 2 ミリメートルのフェルトで作られている]

センチメートル

□ There is a 3- to 4-centimeter-thick layer of clay between limestone layers.
　[石灰層の間に、3 〜 4 センチメートルの厚さの粘土層がある]

メートル

□ The most significant obstacle is mud, which is about two meters thick.
　[最大の障害は泥で、約 2 メートルの厚さがある]

キロメートル

□ Mars' north pole: the cap has an average thickness of one kilometer.
　[火星の北極：氷冠は厚さ平均 1 キロメートルある]

インチ

□ Roll out the dough so it has a thickness of 1 inch.
　[パン生地を麺棒でのばし、厚さ 1 インチにする]
　　＊ 1 inch ＝ 2.54 cm

フィート

□ The walls are three feet thick, with a five-foot-thick roof and a steel door.
　[壁は 3 フィートの厚さで、5 フィートの厚さの屋根と鉄のドアがある]
　　＊ 1 foot ＝ 30.48 cm
　　＊ foot の複数形は feet ですが、five-foot-thick のようにハイフンでつなぐ場合は形容詞となるので、単数の foot を使います。

ヤード

□ This is a picture of 60-yard-thick ice.
　[これは、厚さ 60 ヤードの氷の写真である]

マイル

□ The oceanic crust should be at least 12 miles thick.
　[その海洋地殻は、少なくとも厚さ 12 マイルのはずだ]

24 深さ / 奥行き、厚さ・徹底トレーニング Step 1

1 CDから流れてくる英文を聴き、カッコの部分を書き取ってください。

1) Earth is surrounded by an atmosphere about (   ) km {(   ) miles} deep which protects it from harmful solar radiation and supports all living things.

2) Flatten the dough with the bottom of the pan until it is between (   ) mm and (   ) cm thick.

3) He drilled to a depth of (   ) feet when he reached a rock layer (   ) feet thick.

4) Each bundle must not exceed (   ) feet in length and (   ) feet in thickness.

5) There was a water-filled cavity measuring approximately (   ) m {(   ) ft} deep in the glacier.

解答

1) Earth is surrounded by an atmosphere about (800) km {(500) miles} deep which protects it from harmful solar radiation and supports all living things.
   [地球は、厚さ約800キロメートル（500マイル）の大気に包まれており、それは有害な太陽熱の放射線から地球を守り、すべての生物を支えている]

2) Flatten the dough with the bottom of the pan until it is between (5) mm and (1) cm thick.
   [5ミリメートルから1センチメートルの厚さになるまで、生地を平鍋の底で平らにする]

3) He drilled to a depth of (120) feet when he reached a rock layer (five) feet thick.
   [厚さ5フィートの岩の層に達したとき、彼は120フィートの深さまでドリルで掘っていた]

4) Each bundle must not exceed (4) feet in length and (2) feet in thickness.
   [各包みは、長さ4フィート、厚さ2フィートを超えてはいけない]

5) There was a water-filled cavity measuring approximately (1.4) m {(4.6) ft} deep in the glacier.
   [氷河に、深さ約1.4メートル（4.6フィート）の空洞があり、水がたまっていた]

2TRACK 11

2 CDから流れてくる日本語を聴き、即座に英語に直して発話してください。(＊日本語の後ポーズがあって、その後すぐに英語が流れます)

1)   2)
3)

【解答】
1) 厚さ6ミリメートル   6 mm thick
2) 深さ20フィート   20 feet in depth
3) 奥行き15センチメートル   15 cm deep

3 以下の日本語を英語に直して発話してください。   2TRACK 12

1) 厚さ4メートルの壁

2) 深さ3マイルの海中

3) 地下17メートル

【解答】
1) a four-meter-thick wall
2) three miles deep under water
3) seventeen meters below the ground

高さ、高度（標高、海抜）　Height、Altitude

高さ

ミリメートル

☐ The height of the disc drive is 82 mm.
　［ディスクドライブの高さは、82 ミリメートルだ］

センチメートル

☐ Bee Orchids grow to between 15 and 40 cm high.
　［ミツバチランは、15 ～ 40 センチメートルの高さに成長する］

メートル

☐ That magnificent tower is 18.7 m high.
　［あの荘厳なタワーは、高さ 18.7 メートルだ］

キロメートル

☐ Well-developed thunderclouds can reach heights of up to 19 km.
　［発達した積乱雲は、高さ 19 キロメートルにまで達することがある］
☐ NASA hoped the balloon would circumnavigate the Earth at a height of 35 km.
　［NASA は、気球が高さ 35 キロメートルのところで、地球を 1 周すると見込んでいた］

インチ

☐ The plant grows up to 2 inches high with pale green leaves and yellow flowers in summer.
　［その植物は 2 インチの高さになり、夏には淡緑色の葉と黄色の花をつける］

フィート

☐ The fancy hotel was about 100 feet high.
　　[そのしゃれたホテルは、約 100 フィートの高さだった]

マイル

☐ The world tallest building is about one mile high.
　　[世界で最も高いビルは、高さ約 1 マイルだ]

高度（標高、海抜）

フィート

☐ The present altitude record stands at 79,000 feet.
　　[現在の高度の記録は、79,000 フィートだ]
　　　＊ 1 foot ＝ 30.48 cm
☐ Pressure decreases by 34 millibars every 1,000 feet in altitude.
　　[高度 1,000 フィートごとに、34 ミリバール気圧が低くなる]

メートル

☐ The city center is built on an almost level flood plain just 12 m above sea level.
　　[街の中心は、ちょうど海抜 12 メートルのほぼ平らなはんらん原にある]

キロメートル

☐ The monument stands 1.1 km above sea level on the Harare Plateau.
　　[その記念碑は、ハラレ高原の海抜 1.1 キロメートルのところに建っている]
　　　Harare　ハラレ　＊ジンバブエ共和国の首都

マイル

□ Top tourist attraction Mount Everest is 5.5 miles high.
　［一番の観光名所であるエベレスト山は、標高5.5マイルだ］

25 高さ、高度（標高、海抜）・徹底トレーニング Step 1

1 CD から流れてくる英文を聴き、カッコの部分を書き取ってください。

1) Within a few hours, we arrived at Thimphu, the capital of Bhutan, altitude (　　　) ft.

2) At a height of (　　　) m, they released pairs of (　　　) kg bombs at (　　　)-second intervals.

3) The satellite will orbit over the equator at a height of (　　　) km and closely monitor the tropics.

4) The country's highest historic town is located at over (　　　) feet above sea level.

5) A rocket fired the remains to a height of (　　　) miles {(　　　) km}—the edge of space.

解 答

1) Within a few hours, we arrived at Thimphu, the capital of Bhutan, altitude (8,979) ft.
　　[2〜3時間のうちに、私たちは標高8,979フィートのブータンの首都ティンプーに到着した]

2) At a height of (1,067) m, they released pairs of (1,000) kg bombs at (five)-second intervals.
　　[高度1,067メートルのところで、彼らは5秒の間隔で1,000キログラム2個セットの爆弾を、何発も投下した]

3) The satellite will orbit over the equator at a height of (867) km and closely monitor the tropics.
　　[その衛星は、赤道上高さ867キロメートルの軌道を回り、熱帯地方を注意深く監視する]

4) The country's highest historic town is located at over (1,000) feet above sea level.
　　[その国の最も標高が高い歴史的な街は、海抜 1,000 フィート以上のところに位置している]

5) A rocket fired the remains to a height of (72.7) miles {(117) km}—the edge of space.
　　[高さ 72.7 マイル（117 キロメートル）の宇宙空間で、ロケットは残骸を落とした]

　　　　　　　　　　　　　　　　　　　　　　　　　　　🎧 2TRACK 14

2 CD から流れてくる日本語を聴き、即座に英語に直して発話してください。（＊日本語の後ポーズがあって、その後すぐに英語が流れます）

1)
2)
3)

【解　答】

1) 高さ 4.5 メートル　　　　　4.5 m high
2) 高さ 30 フィート　　　　　30 feet in height
3) 18 キロメートルの高さ　　　a height of 18 km

3　以下の日本語を英語に直して発話してください。　🎧 2TRACK 15

1) 高さ 1.5 メートルのフェンス

2) 高さ 2.1 メートル以下の乗り物

3) 高さ 309 フィートの塔

【解　答】

1) the 1.5-meter-high fence
2) vehicles under 2.1 m high
3) the 309-foot-high tower

面積、容積 / 体積　Area、Volume

面　積

平方ミリメートル

☐ The board space is 80 mm².
　　［基板面積は、80 平方ミリメートルだ］
　　　　＊ mm² = square millimeter

平方センチメートル

☐ Logos should be restricted to 26 sq.cm.
　　［ロゴは、26 平方センチメートルに限定されている］
　　　　＊ sq.cm = square centimeter = cm²

平方メートル

☐ A deluxe three-bedroom, 150 sq.m apartment
　　［豪華な3つの寝室付き、150 平方メートルのアパート］
　　　　＊ sq.m = square meter = m²

平方キロメートル

☐ The facilities are located in the 1,325 sq.km National Park.
　　［その施設は、1,325 平方キロメートルの国立公園内にある］
　　　　＊ sq.km = square kilometer = km²

平方インチ

☐ The steam pressure was 150 lb per square inch.
　　［蒸気圧は、1 平方インチあたり 150 ポンドだった］
　　　　＊ square inch = sq.in. = in²
　　　　＊ lb = libra（ラテン語）　重さの単位、ポンドを表す記号。ポンドと読みます。

平方フィート

☐ The company is putting up a 1.2 million-square-foot distribution center.
　　［その会社は、120 万平方フィートの流通センターを建設中だ］
　　　＊ square foot = sq.ft. = ft²　　＊ 1 sq.ft. = 0.093 m² = 0.028 坪

平方ヤード

☐ My present garden is 250 square yards of bumpy, weed-infested pastureland.
　　［私の庭は現在、250 平方ヤードのでこぼこの多い雑草の生い茂った放牧地になっている］
　　　＊ square yard = sq. yd. = yd²　　＊ 1 sq.yd. ≒ 0.84 m²

ヘクタール

☐ The hospital will be situated on a 16-hectare site.
　　［その病院は、16 ヘクタールの敷地に建てられることになる］
　　　＊ 1 hectare = 10,000 m²

エーカー

☐ The family has been on the 4,000-acre estate for 146 years.
　　［その一族は、4,000 エーカーの土地に 146 年間住んでいる］
　　　＊ 1 acre ≒ 4,047 m² ≒ 1,224 坪

平方マイル

☐ One warship was trying to cover an area of more than a million square miles.
　　［1 隻の戦艦が、100 万平方マイル以上の領域を、カバーしようとしていた］
　　　＊ square mile = sq.mi. = mi²　　＊ 1 sq.mi ≒ 2.6 km²

四方

☐ Cut the clay into cubes about 2 cm square.
　　［粘土を、約 2 センチメートル四方の立方体にカットする］

容積 / 体積

ミリリットル

☐ The pilgrims were told they could not carry holy water in bottles bigger than 100 milliliters.
　　［巡礼者は、100 ミリリットルよりも大きいボトルで聖水を運んではいけない、と言われていた］

リットル

☐ This car wash device enables the car user to wash the car with less than 3 liters of water.
　　［この洗車装置によって、車の使用者は 3 リットル以下の水で車を洗うことができる］

キロリットル

☐ They may consume 65 million kiloliters of fuel this year.
　　［彼らは今年、6,500 万キロリットルの燃料を消費するかもしれない］

オンス

☐ Pour in 10 fl oz of lukewarm water.
　　［10（液量）オンスの、なまぬるい水を注ぐ］
　　　＊ fl oz = fluid ounce(s) ＝液量オンス　　＊ 1 fl oz ≒ 30 ml

パイント

☐ The price of a pint of beer could be going up in the near future.
　［近い将来、ビール 1 パイントの値段が上がるかもしれない］
　　＊ pint = pt.　＊ 1 pint = 1/8 gallon ≒ 500 ml

クォート

☐ You can't get a quart into a pint pot.
　［容量 1 パイントのポットに、1 クォートの容量のものを入れることはできない（比喩）。→無理なことをしている］
　　＊ quart = qt.　＊ 1 quart = 2 pints = 1/4 gallon

バレル

☐ Oil prices have fallen to $125 per barrel.
　［石油の価格は、1 バレルあたり 125 ドルに下がった］
　　＊ barrel = bbl. / bl.
　　＊ 1 barrel ≒（石油用）159 liters、（用途によらない標準の液量）119 litlers

ガロン

☐ We have about 600 gallons of water.
　［私たちには、約 600 ガロンの水がある］
　　＊ 1 gallon = 8 pints ≒ 3.8 liters

立方センチメートル

☐ If the size of the engine is over 1,000 cc, competitors are fined.
　［エンジンのサイズが 1,000 cc 以上だった場合、競技者は罰金を科せられる］

立方メートル

□ One drop of oil is sufficient to contaminate one cubic meter of drinking water, making it undrinkable.
　［たった1滴の石油で、1立方メートルの飲料水が十分汚染され、飲めなくなってしまう］
　　＊ cubic meter ＝ m^3

立方ヤード

□ An astonishing five million cubic yards of snow were removed from the road.
　［500万立方ヤードの驚くほどの雪が、道路から取り除かれた］
　　＊ 1 cubic yard (cu. yd.) ＝ 27 ft^3 ≒ 0.7646 m^3

立方インチ

□ That American car had a 312-cubic-inch engine in it.
　［そのアメリカの車は、312立方インチのエンジンを搭載していた］
　　＊ cubic inch ＝ cu.in. ＝ in^3

立方フィート

□ The size of the structure is 2,900,000 cubic feet.
　［その建造物のサイズは、290万立方フィートだ］
□ A cubic foot of copper weighs 559 lb.
　［1立方フィートの銅は、重さ559ポンドだ］
　　＊ cubic foot と cubic feet の両方を使いますが、日本語ではどちらも「フィート」と訳します。

26 面積、容積/体積・徹底トレーニング Step 1

1 CDから流れてくる英文を聴き、カッコの部分を書き取ってください。

1) The South Bank is building a ( )-story, ( )-square-foot headquarters on its property.

2) Almost half of the continent of Africa, about ( ) square km, is covered by savannah.

3) Its density is approximately ( ) grams per cubic centimeter {( ) ounces per cubic inch}.

4) Sow your lawn seed at ( ) oz per square yard {( ) gm per square meter}.

5) It is a metric unit of volume equal to ( ) liters {( ) liquid quarts}.

6) Each barrel contained ( ) pints {( ) liters} of beer.

7) The Commission called for an increase in the size of battery hen cages from ( ) sq.cm minimum floor area to ( ) sq.cm.

8) They plan to buy up to ( ) billion cubic meters of natural gas a year. A further ( ) billion cubic meters will be sold to European countries.

9) We asked him to include a ( )-square-kilometer {( )-acre} area in the scheme.

10) Pour ( ) liters of water into the ( )-liter bucket.

解 答

1) The South Bank is building a (two)-story, (8,000)-square-foot headquarters on its property.
   [サウス銀行は、2階建、床面積 8,000 平方フィートの本社ビルを、自社所有地に建設中だ]

2) Almost half of the continent of Africa, about (13 million) square km, is covered by savannah.
   [アフリカ大陸のほぼ半分にあたる、約 1,300 万平方キロメートルは、サバンナが占めている]

3) Its density is approximately (2.7) grams per cubic centimeter {(1.55) ounces per cubic inch}.
   [その密度は、1 立方センチメートルにつき約 2.7 グラム（1 立方インチにつき 1.55 オンス）だ]

4) Sow your lawn seed at (1) oz per square yard {(35) gm per square meter}.
   [1 平方ヤードにつき、1 オンス（1 平方メートルにつき 35 グラム）の芝の種をまきなさい]

5) It is a metric unit of volume equal to (1,000) liters {(1,056) liquid quarts)}.
   [それは、メートル法の体積 1,000 リットル（1,056 液量クォート）に相当する]

6) Each barrel contained (72) pints {(41) liters} of beer.
   [それぞれの樽には、72 パイント（41 リットル）のビールが入っていた]

7) The Commission called for an increase in the size of battery hen cages from (450) sq.cm minimum floor area to (800) sq.cm.
   [委員会は、雌鶏用ケージの最低床面積を 450 平方センチメートルから 800 平方センチメートルに増やすことを要求した]

8) They plan to buy up to (sixteen) billion cubic meters of natural gas a year. A further (fourteen) billion cubic meters will be sold to European countries.
   [彼らは、1 年に 160 億立方メートルまでの天然ガスを買い占め、さらに 140 億立方メートルをヨーロッパの国々に販売するつもりだ]

9) We asked him to include a (371)-square-kilometer {(91,676)-acre} area in the scheme.
   [私たちは、その計画に 371 平方キロメートル（91,676 エーカー）のエリアを含めるよう、彼に要請した]

10) Pour (3) liters of water into the (4)-liter bucket.
    [3 リットルの水を、4 リットルバケツに入れなさい]

8 単位

🎧 2TRACK 17

2 CD から流れてくる日本語を聴き、即座に英語に直して発話してください。（＊日本語の後ポーズがあって、その後すぐに英語が流れます）

1)   2)
3)   4)
5)

解答

1) 13 リットル   13 l.
2) 1.5 オンス   1.5 ounces
3) 50 平方キロメートル 50 sq.km
4) 275 ミリリットル   275 ml
5) 80 キロリットル   80 kl

3 以下の日本語を英語に直して発話してください。 🎧 2TRACK 18

1) 2 バレルのビール

2) 1,000 立方メートルの海水

3) 83 平方キロメートルの包装紙

4) 1 クォートサイズの水差し

5) 500 平方メートルの地域

解 答

1) 2 barrels of beer
2) 1,000 cubic meters of sea water
3) 83 square km of wrapping paper
4) a quart-size jar
5) a 500-square-meter area

距離、速度、角度　Distance、Speed、Angle

距　離

メートル

☐ We saw one bird about 15-20 meters away from us.
　　［私たちは、約 15〜20 メートル離れたところに、1 羽の鳥を見た］

キロメートル

☐ His hometown is about 900 km southwest of Tokyo.
　　［彼の故郷は、東京の南西約 900 キロメートルのところにある］

マイル

☐ I've been running 3-4 miles on weekday mornings.
　　［私は平日の朝、3〜4 マイル走っている］
　　　＊ 1 mile ＝ 1,760 yards ＝ 1,609.344 m ≒ 1.6 km

ブロック

☐ My office is 4 blocks from my house.
　　［私の事務所は、私の家から 4 ブロック先にある］

速　度

秒速

☐ My home computer writes at four megabytes per second.
　　［私の家庭用コンピュータは、1 秒間に 4 メガバイトで書き込む］

分速

☐ That model runs at 1 mile per minute.
   [そのモデルは、分速 1 マイルで走る]

時速

☐ Category 5 storm winds are faster than 250 km/h.
   [カテゴリー 5 のハリケーンの風速は、時速 250 キロメートルを超える]
☐ The police estimated the motorbike's speed at between 105 and 119 mph.
   [警官は、そのバイクのスピードは、時速 105 〜 119 マイルと推定した]
   ＊ mph ＝ mile(s) per hour

マッハ

☐ The supersonic aircraft is designed to accelerate to between Mach 7 and Mach 10 — seven to ten times the speed of sound.
   [超音速機は、マッハ 7 〜 10 に加速するように設計されている—音速の 7 〜 10 倍の速さである]
   ＊ 1 mach ＝ 1,225 km/h

ノット

☐ The ship was moving at around 8.5 knots.
   [その船は、約 8.5 ノットで進んでいた]
   ＊ 1 knot ＝ 1.852 km/h

回転

☐ Wind turbines generally have 3 blades and they rotate at 10-30 revolutions per minute.
   [風力タービンは、通常、3 枚の羽で 1 分間に 10 〜 30 回転する]
   ＊ revolutions per minute ＝ r.p.m

角 度

角 度

☐ A narrow boat became stuck between the rocks at a 40-degree angle.
　［細いボートが、40度の角度で岩間に挟まって動かなくなった］

勾 配

☐ The stadium's stand has a gradient of more than 30 degrees.
　［スタジアムのスタンドは、30度以上の勾配だ］

27 距離、速度、角度・徹底トレーニング Step 1

1 CD から流れてくる英文を聴き、カッコの部分を書き取ってください。

1) In the early (　　　) we moved approximately (　　　) miles to another small village.

2) Shanghai is still (　　　) km away, but after travelling (　　　) km, a couple of hundred kilometers seems close enough to see from here.

3) Skeleton speeds approach (　　　) mph {(　　　) km/h}.

4) Italy is one of the few places in the world where you can go (　　　) miles away and eat something completely different.

5) There were (　　) or (　　) houses burning (　　　) meters away from home.

6) A gang's turf used to cover an area of (　　　) to (　　　) blocks. Today, it's more like (　　　) to (　　　) blocks.

7) The object that looked like a UFO turned at a (　　　)-degree angle, then suddenly stopped, and we watched it for a good (　　　) hours.

8) The hurricane continues to move to the west-northwest, now more than (　　) miles northeast of the island, with winds near (　　　) mph.

9) The server was a little bit slower — with a minimum of (　　　) MB per second and a maximum of (　　　) MB per second.

10) The carriage tilted at something like a (　　　)-degree angle. Our particular carriage was at about a (　　　)-degree angle.

解　答

1) In the early (1950s) we moved approximately (8) miles to another small village.
　　［1950年代の初め、私たちは約8マイル離れた小さな村へ引っ越した］

2) Shanghai is still (230) km away, but after travelling (17,700) km, a couple of hundred kilometers seems close enough to see from here.
　　［上海まではあと230キロメートル、でも今まで旅してきた17,700キロメートルを思えば、数百キロメートルというのはもうここから目に見えるほどの距離だ］

3) Skeleton speeds approach (84) mph {(135) km/h}.
　　［スケルトンのスピードは、時速84マイル（時速135キロメートル）近くにまで達する］

4) Italy is one of the few places in the world where you can go (10 to 20) miles away and eat something completely different.
　　［イタリアは、10～20マイル離れた場所でまったく異なる料理が味わえる、世界でも数少ない国の1つだ］

5) There were (2) or (3) houses burning (500) meters away from home.
　　［自宅から500メートルの所で、2～3軒の家が燃えていた］

6) A gang's turf used to cover an area of (five) to (ten) blocks. Today, it's more like (two) to (three) blocks.
　　［ギャングはかつて5～10ブロックを支配していたものだったが、今や2～3ブロックだ］

7) The object that looked like a UFO turned at a (45)-degree angle, then suddenly stopped, and we watched it for a good (2) hours.
　　［そのUFOのような物体は、角度45度になって突然止まった。われわれは、それを2時間たっぷり見ていた］

8) The hurricane continues to move to the west-northwest, now more than (610) miles northeast of the island, with winds near (135) mph.
　　［ハリケーンは西北西へ移動を続け、現在島の北東610マイルにまで達する。風速は、時速135マイル近い］

9) The server was a little bit slower — with a minimum of (1) MB per second and a maximum of (3.9) MB per second.
　　［そのサーバーは（他に比べて）少し遅かった—最低秒速 1 メガバイトで、最高秒速 3.9 メガバイトだった］
　　　＊ MB = megabyte

10) The carriage tilted at something like a (40)-degree angle. Our particular carriage was at about a (45)-degree angle.
　　［その台車は約 40 度傾いた。そして、他ならぬわれわれの台車は、約 45 度の傾きだった］

🄯 2TRACK 20

2 CD から流れてくる日本語を聴き、即座に英語に直して発話してください。（＊日本語の後ポーズがあって、その後すぐに英語が流れます）

1)　　　　　　　　　　　　2)
3)　　　　　　　　　　　　4)
5)

【解　答】

1)　90 マイル　　　　　　　90 miles
2)　時速 75 キロ　　　　　　75 km/h
3)　5〜6 ブロック　　　　　5 or 6 blocks
4)　角度 30 度　　　　　　　30-degree angle
5)　78 キロメートル　　　　78 km

3 以下の日本語を英語に直して発話してください。　🄯 2TRACK 21

1)　3.5 キロメートルの運転

2)　70 ヤード離れたところ

3)　時速 40 マイル制限

4)　秒速 50 メガビット

182

5) 通常の潮の 7 メートル以上

[解 答]
1) a 3.5-kilometer drive
2) 70 yards away
3) a 40-mph limit
4) 50 Mbps 　（megabits per second）
5) more than 7 meters above the normal tide

緯度、経度　Latitude、Longitude

～度、～分、～秒

□ Tokyo lies at 140° east longitude and 36° north latitude.
　［東京は東経140度、北緯36度に位置している］
□ An area of ocean at forty-seven degrees south latitude and one hundred-and-forty degrees west longitude
　［南緯47度と西経140度の海域］
□ A typical latitude might be 52°30'25" N.
　［一般的に緯度は、北緯52度30分25秒のように表す］
□ People visit Greenwich to see the 0° longitude line which is known as the Prime Meridian.
　［本初子午線として知られている、経度0度の線を見るために、人々はグリニッジを訪れる］

　　　Prime Meridian　本初子午線、グリニッジ子午線
　　＊ Greenwich Meridian とも言います。

28 緯度、経度・徹底トレーニング Step 1

1 CDから流れてくる英文を聴き、カッコの部分を書き取ってください。

1) The radar system can collect high-resolution images of the Earth's crust between (　　) degrees north latitude and (　　) degrees south latitude.

2) Water lies between the Equator and (　　) south latitude, and east of (　　) east longitude.

3) Longitude lines run from top to bottom, measured in (　　) east and west with the Greenwich Meridian at (　　).

4) He was travelling longitude west (　　) degrees.

5) The splashdown footprint centers roughly around (　　) degrees south latitude and (　　) degrees west longitude.

解 答

1) The radar system can collect high-resolution images of the Earth's crust between (60) degrees north latitude and (56) degrees south latitude.
　［そのレーダーシステムで、北緯60度と南緯56度の間にある地殻の高解像度画像を集めることができる］

2) Water lies between the Equator and (6°00') south latitude, and east of (3°00') east longitude.
　［その海は、赤道から南緯6度00分、東経3度00分より東に位置している］

3) Longitude lines run from top to bottom, measured in (180°) east and west with the Greenwich Meridian at (zero).
　［経線は南北にのびて、経度0度のグリニッジ子午線から、東西に180度まである］

4) He was travelling longitude west (135) degrees.
　［彼は、西経135度を旅行していた］

5) The splashdown footprint centers roughly around (44) degrees south latitude and (150) degrees west longitude.
　　［着水地点は、約南緯44度、西経150度に集中している］

🎧 2TRACK 23

2 CDから流れてくる日本語を聴き、即座に英語に直して発話してください。（＊日本語の後ポーズがあって、その後すぐに英語が流れます）

1)　　　　　　　　　　　2)
3)

【解　答】

1) 南緯35度　　　　　　　35 degrees south latitude
2) 東経138度　　　　　　138 degrees east longitude
3) 北緯23度5分　　　　　23 degrees 5 minutes north latitude

3 以下の日本語を英語に直して発話してください。　🎧 2TRACK 24

1) 北極圏―北緯66度30分

2) （北緯）38度線

3) 本初子午線（経度0度）

【解　答】

1) the Arctic Circle ― 66°30' N.
2) the 38th parallel
3) the Prime Meridian (longitude 0 degrees)

気象　Meteorology

温度、湿度

☐ You can expect hot sunshine, 28°C and 53% humidity today.
　　[今日は日差しが照りつけ、摂氏28度、湿度53％になるだろう]
　　　　C = centigrade / Celsius　摂氏

☐ Today was extremely hot, as it got up to 90 degrees F.
　　[今日はとても暑く、気温が華氏90度まで上がった]
　　　　F = Fahrenheit　華氏
　　　　＊摂氏と華氏の換算式は（°F − 32）× 5/9 = °C ですが、°F ÷ 2 − 15 = °C でもほぼ同じ数字が出ます。

マグニチュード

☐ An earthquake with a magnitude of 6.3 on the Ricter scale struck a sparsely populated area in China yesterday.
　　[昨日、中国の人口まばらな地域でマグニチュード6.3の地震が起きた]
　　　　＊「震度」は、日本の気象庁が震度計による観測値に基づいて発表する数値で、Japanese seismic intensity といいます。
　　　　例）Japanese seismic intensity (scale of) 5、intensity 5「震度5」
　　　　＊ Ricter scale　リヒタースケール（マグニチュード表示用）

降水量、降水確率

☐ Flooding occurred after a reported 100 mm (4 inches) of rain fell in the area.
　　[（1時間に）100ミリメートル（4インチ）の雨が降ったという報道の後、その地域に洪水が起こった]
　　　　＊ 1 inch = 2.54 cm

☐ There is about a 70% chance of rain on Thursday.
　　[木曜日の降水確率は、約70%だ]
　　　　＊降水確率は、chance of precipitation ともいいます。

風　速

☐ Wind speeds can reach 300 miles per hour.
　　［風速は、時速 300 マイルに達することもある］
　　　＊風速は、wind velocity、velocity of wind ともいいます。
　　　＊ miles per hour ＝ mph

気　圧

☐ 1 mb is equal to 1 hPa or 100 Pa.
　　［1 ミリバールは 1 ヘクトパスカル、すなわち 100 パスカルである］
　　　＊ mb ＝ mbar ＝ millibar、hPa ＝ hectopascal、Pa ＝ pascal は圧力単位です。
☐ At sea level the amount of oxygen in the air is about 21% with a pressure of 760 mmHg.
　　［海面では空気中の酸素は約 21%、気圧は 760 ミリ水銀だ］
　　　＊ mmHg（ミリメートル水銀柱）は、圧力単位です。
　　　＊通常、物理学では「ミリ水銀」、医療では「ミリメートルエイチジー」と読みます。

29 気象・徹底トレーニング Step 1

1 CDから流れてくる英文を聴き、カッコの部分を書き取ってください。

1) The largest quake recorded anywhere this year was a magnitude (　　) in Hokkaido, Japan.

2) Weather forecasters say there is a (　　)% chance of rain with showers likely to be heavy with thunderstorms.

3) The average pressure at sea level is (　　) millibars.

4) The seismologist said yesterday's quake had a magnitude of (　　), compared with the quake in (　　) which was (　　).

5) Temperatures vary from (　　)°C to (　　)°C, but can be much lower in the highlands.

解答

1) The largest quake recorded anywhere this year was a magnitude (8.3) in Hokkaido, Japan.
   [今年記録された最大の地震は、マグニチュード8.3の日本の北海道で起こったものであった]

2) Weather forecasters say there is a (40)% chance of rain with showers likely to be heavy with thunderstorms.
   [気象予報士は、降水確率は40%で、雷とどしゃぶりのにわか雨を伴うもようだと言っている]

3) The average pressure at sea level is (1,013.25) millibars.
   [海面平均気圧は、1,013.25ミリバールである]

4) The seismologist said yesterday's quake had a magnitude of (2.8), compared with the quake in (2007) which was (4.3).
   [地震学者は、2007年の地震がマグニチュード4.3だったのに対し、昨日の地震はマグニチュード2.8だったと発表した]

5) Temperatures vary from (24)°C to (30)°C, but can be much lower in the highlands.
　　［気温は摂氏 24 〜 30 度までさまざまだが、山岳地方ではそれよりずっと低い可能性がある］

　　　＊ °C の C や °F の F は、どうしてもそれがないと理解できない場合を除いて、通常、口語では省略されます。記載する際も、省略されて「°」あるいは degrees のみの場合があります。

🎧 2TRACK 26

2 CD から流れてくる日本語を聴き、即座に英語に直して発話してください。（＊日本語の後ポーズがあって、その後すぐに英語が流れます）

1)　　　　　　　　　　2)
3)

解 答

1) 華氏 83 度　　　　　　83°F
2) 摂氏 19 度　　　　　　19°C
3) 湿度 40%　　　　　　40% humidity

3 以下の日本語を英語に直して発話してください。　🎧 2TRACK 27

1) 今夜：概ね晴れ、最低気温：華氏 69 度 / 摂氏 21 度

2) マグニチュード 5.6 の地震

3) 気圧：29.94 mmHg

解 答

1) Tonight: mainly clear, Low: 69°F / 21°C
2) a 5.6-magnitude earthquake
3) Barometer: 29.94 mmHg
　　　barometer　気圧計

9 さらに徹底トレーニング
Extra Training

🔊 2TRACK 28

30 時間・徹底トレーニング Step 2

1 CDから流れてくる英文を聴き、カッコの部分を書き取ってください。

1) Details on the (　　) (　　)-minute films cover the main agenda items for the World Summit on the Environment.

2) Hours: dinner: Sun-Tue: (　　)-(　　) pm, Wed-Thu: (　　)-(　　) pm, Fri-Sat: (　　)-(　　) pm; Lounge: Mon-Thu (　　) pm-(　　) am, Fri-Sat: (　　) pm-(　　) am.

3) After a (　　) to (　　)-minute drive into the city, we had a (　　)-minute brief on up-to-date issues and then grabbed a coffee.

4) Page last updated at (　　) GMT, Thursday, (　　) September, (　　) (　　) U.K.

5) This section has (　　) timelines. The first shows details of the period from (　　) BC until the end of the Greek empire in (　　) BC.

6) They released additional duo albums in (　　) and (　　), reunited as a duo for a (　　) album, and continued to play concerts together.

解答

1) Details on the (six) (ten)-minute films cover the main agenda items for the World Summit on the Environment.
　　[6本ある10分間の映像の詳細は、世界環境サミットの主要議題項目を扱っている]

191

2) Hours: dinner: Sun-Tue: (5:30)-(9) pm, Wed-Thu: (5:30)-(10) pm, Fri-Sat: (5:30)-(11) pm; Lounge: Mon-Thu (5) pm-(1:30) am, Fri-Sat: (5) pm-(2:30) am.
[営業時間：ディナー：日 - 火：5:30-9 pm, 水 - 木：5:30-10 pm, 金 - 土：5:30-11 pm；ラウンジ：月 - 木 5 pm-1:30 am, 金 - 土：5 pm-2:30 am]

3) After a (twenty) to (thirty)-minute drive into the city, we had a (ten)-minute brief on up-to-date issues and then grabbed a coffee.
[われわれは 20 〜 30 分間車を運転して街へ入ると、最近の話題について軽く 10 分ほど話し、それからコーヒーを飲んだ]

4) Page last updated at (13:35) GMT, Thursday, (25) September, (2008) (14:35) U.K.
[ページ最終更新は 2008 年 9 月 25 日木曜日、グリニッジ標準時 13 時 35 分。英国標準時 14 時 35 分]

5) This section has (two) timelines. The first shows details of the period from (800) BC until the end of the Greek empire in (146) BC.
[このセクションには、2 つの年代記がある。1 つ目には、紀元前 800 年から紀元前 146 年のギリシャ帝国の終わりまでの詳細が示されている]

6) They released additional duo albums in (1971) and (1975), reunited as a duo for a (1994) album, and continued to play concerts together.
[彼らは、さらに 1971 年と 1975 年にデュオでアルバムをリリースした。1994 年にはデュオを再結成して 1 枚のアルバムを出し、その後も一緒にコンサート活動を続けた]

🔘 2TRACK 29

2 CD から流れてくる日本語を聴き、即座に英語に直して発話してください。(*日本語の後ポーズがあって、その後すぐに英語が流れます)

1) 　　　　　　　　　　2)
3) 　　　　　　　　　　4)
5)

解 答

1) （西暦）2000 年　　　2000 A.D.
2) 午後 5 時 20 分過ぎ　　5:20 pm　(twenty past / after five、five twenty)
3) 8 時 7 分前　　　　　　7:53　(seven to / before / of eight)

4)	年中無休の店	a 24 / 7 store
5)	12 時ちょうど	twelve o'clock sharp

3 以下の日本語を英語に直して発話してください。　2TRACK 30

1) 1970～80 年代のウッドストックで

2) 観測時刻：2008 年 9 月 6 日土曜日正午

3) 最新の交通、運行ニュース― 24 時間 7 日間アップデート

4) 1 位：1 時間 00 分 39 秒

5) 30 分に 1 回から、1 時間に 1 回に減らす。

解答

1) in Woodstock during the 1970s and '80s
2) Observed: Saturday Sept. 6, 2008 at 12:00 pm
3) The latest traffic and travel news — updated 24-7
4) 1st: 1 hour 00 minute 39 seconds
5) Reduce from once every half-hour to once an hour.

31 年齢・徹底トレーニング Step 2

1 CDから流れてくる英文を聴き、カッコの部分を書き取ってください。

1) Census figures from (　　) show that (　　) percent of women between the ages of (　　) and (　　) had (　　) child.

2) The primary engine of decades of sustained growth in foreign travel has been the Japanese woman, aged (　　) to (　　).

3) The sleep your child needs will fall from (　　) hours a night at (　　) years old to (　　) by age (　　).

4) Nearly (　　) of children placed in the facility in (　　) were (　　) years old or younger.

5) The divorce rate among the over-(　　) has risen dramatically in the last (　　) years.

6) Intrauterine insemination, or IUI, led to pregnancy in (　　) percent of women under (　　), but just (　　) percent in older women.

7) Actors required for short film: female {mid-(　　) - mid-(　　)}, male / female {(　　) - (　　) years old)}

解答

1) Census figures from (2004) show that (17.4) percent of women between the ages of (40) and (44) had (one) child.
　　[2004年の国勢調査によると、40～44歳の女性の17.4%が子どもは1人だった]

2) The primary engine of decades of sustained growth in foreign travel has been the Japanese woman, aged (20) to (29).
　　[海外旅行において、何十年もの持続的成長の第一原動力となっているのは、20～29歳までの日本人女性だった]

3) The sleep your child needs will fall from (11.5) hours a night at (four) years old to (10.5) by age (seven).
   [子どもが必要とする睡眠時間は、4歳の一晩11.5時間から、7歳までには10.5時間に減る]

4) Nearly (two-thirds) of children placed in the facility in (2007) were (10) years old or younger.
   [2007年に、その施設に預けられた子どものほぼ3分の2が、10歳以下だった]

5) The divorce rate among the over-(50s) has risen dramatically in the last (20) years.
   [50代以上の離婚率は、過去20年間で劇的に上昇している]

6) Intrauterine insemination, or IUI, led to pregnancy in (14.5) percent of women under (35), but just (8.9) percent in older women.
   [子宮内授精（IUI）の場合、35歳未満の女性は14.5％が妊娠したが、35歳以上ではわずか8.9％だった]

7) Actors required for short film: female {mid-(20s) - mid-(30s)}, male / female {(10) - (13) years old)}
   [短編映画の俳優募集：女性（20代半ば～30代半ば）、男性/女性（10～13歳）]

2TRACK 32

2 CDから流れてくる日本語を聴き、即座に英語に直して発話してください。（＊日本語の後ポーズがあって、その後すぐに英語が流れます）

1)   2)
3)   4)
5)

解答

1) 年齢40～49歳　　　　　ages 40 to 49
2) 10代の若者たち　　　　teenagers
3) 50歳未満　　　　　　　below the age of 50
4) 樹齢1,200年の木　　　　a 1,200 year-old tree
5) 年齢30代の女性たち　　women in their thirties

3 以下の日本語を英語に直して発話してください。　🎧 2TRACK 33

1）私は50代半ばの、生粋のブルックリン住民だ。

2）12〜16歳の若者向けサポートサービス

3）私の父は、77歳まで働いた。

4）18歳未満入場お断り

5）彼は、年齢を4歳さばを読んでいた。

解答

1) I am a native Brooklynite in my mid-fifties.
　　Brooklynite （ニューヨーク）ブルックリン人、ブルックリン住民
　　＊ちなみに、「東京都民、東京人」は Tokyoite、「大阪府民、大阪人」は Osakan、「名古屋市民、名古屋人」は Nagoyan、「沖縄県民、沖縄人」は Okinawan といいます。
2) Support services for young people between 12 and 16 years old
3) My father worked until he was 77 years old.
4) No admission to persons under 18 / under the age of 18
5) He knocked four years off his age.

32 通貨、為替・徹底トレーニング Step 2

1 CDから流れてくる英文を聴き、カッコの部分を書き取ってください。

1) The pound was trading at $(　　), as against $(　　) at the previous close.

2) He was given a choice of (　　) year in jail or to pay a fine of €(　　) equivalent to just over £(　　).

3) U.S.$(　　) was (　　) old Zimbabwean dollars {(　　) new Zimbabwean dollars} but now you need (　　) new Zimbabwean dollars to buy (　　) U.S. dollar.

4) The Canadian parliament passed a CAD (　　) bn {$(　　) bn; £(　　) bn} economic stimulus package.

5) The rupiah is trading at (　　) to the dollar, compared to only (　　) (　　) days ago and (　　) at the beginning of the year.

6) The cost was roughly equivalent to ¥(　　) {£(　　)} for every Japanese man, woman and child.

7) One of the world's rarest coins, an (　　) silver US dollar worth at least $(　　), has been found.

解答

1) The pound was trading at $(1.479), as against $(1.483) at the previous close.
　　[1ポンドは、前日終値の1.483ドルに対して1.479ドルで取引されていた]

2) He was given a choice of (one) year in jail or to pay a fine of €(3,100) equivalent to just over £(2,000).
　　[彼は1年間刑務所に入るか、それとも2,000ポンドを少し上回る金額に相当する3,100ユーロの罰金の支払いかの選択が与えられた]

3) U.S.$(1) was (100,000) old Zimbabwean dollars {(100) new Zimbabwean dollars} but now you need (250) new Zimbabwean dollars to buy (one) U.S. dollar.
　　[1米ドルは、10万旧ジンバブエドル（100新ジンバブエドル）だったが、現在は1ドル購入するのに、250新ジンバブエドルが必要だ]
　　Zimbabwean dollar　ジンバブエの通貨単位・ドル

4) The Canadian parliament passed a CAD (40) bn {$(32) bn; £(23) bn} economic stimulus package.
　　[カナダ議会は、400億カナダドル（320億米ドル；230億ポンド）の景気刺激策法案を通過させた]

5) The rupiah is trading at (6,000) to the dollar, compared to only (4,000) (ten) days ago and (2,350) at the beginning of the year.
　　[今年の初めに1ドル2,350ルピア、10日前は4,000ルピアだったのに対し、現在は6,000ルピアで取引されている]
　　rupiah　インドネシアの通貨単位・ルピア

6) The cost was roughly equivalent to ¥(200,000) {£(1,089)} for every Japanese man, woman and child.
　　[その費用は、日本人すべての男女、および子どもに対し、おおよそ20万円（1,089ポンド）の負担に相当した]

7) One of the world's rarest coins, an (1866) silver US dollar worth at least $(1m), has been found.
　　[世界で最も珍しいコインの1つで、少なくとも100万ドルの価値がある1866年発行の米ドル銀貨が発見された]

🎧 2TRACK 35

2　CDから流れてくる日本語を聴き、即座に英語に直して発話してください。(＊日本語の後ポーズがあって、その後すぐに英語が流れます)

1)　　　　　　　　　　　2)
3)　　　　　　　　　　　4)
5)

解答

1)　一万円札10枚　　　　　　ten ten-thousand yen bills
2)　500ユーロ紙幣3枚　　　　three five-hundred-euro notes

3) 25セント硬貨6枚　　　six quarters
4) 10ペンス硬貨2枚　　　two ten-pence pieces、two ten pees
5) 8,000ドル　　　　　　eight grand、eight thousand dollars

3　以下の日本語を英語に直して発話してください。　2TRACK 36

1) ポンド高となり、1ドル1.62ポンドになった。

2) 終値1ドル44.69ルピーで引けた。

3) 1ポンド1.26ユーロの為替レート

4) 為替相場で、1ポンドは1ドル99セント以上に上昇した。

5) ドルは、1ユーロ1ドル23セントに下落した。

解答

1) The pound strengthened to 1.62 against the dollar.
2) The rupee closed at 44.69 against the dollar.
　　　rupee　インド・パキスタン・スリランカなどの通貨単位・ルピー
3) an exchange rate of £1 to €1.26
4) The pound rose above $1.99 on currency exchanges.
5) The dollar slid to 1.23 to the euro.

33 株式、債券・徹底トレーニング Step 2

🎧 2TRACK 37

1 CDから流れてくる英文を聴き、カッコの部分を書き取ってください。

1) Car phone shares closed at (　　) pence, (　　)% or (　　) pence below the offer price of (　　) pence.

2) The benchmark (　　)-issue Nikkei Stock Average rose (　　) points, or (　　)%, to close at (　　).

3) Google share prices rose by (　　)%, rising to $(　　) {£(　　)}, while Yahoo rose (　　)% to $(　　) {£(　　)}.

4) The company's share price reportedly rose from (　　) yuan a share in late (　　) to more than (　　) yuan in February (　　).

5) The gaming product company's share price surged on the news, rising (　　) yen, or (　　)%, to (　　) yen on the Tokyo Stock Exchange.

6) The benchmark Dow Jones Average plunged below (　　) points with a tumble of (　　) points {(　　) percent} to (　　) and the NASDAQ slumped (　　) points {(　　) percent} to (　　).

解答

1) Car phone shares closed at (192) pence, (4)% or (8) pence below the offer price of (200) pence.
   [自動車電話株は、192ペンスで引けた。それは公募価格の200ペンスよりも4%、8ペンス安だった]

2) The benchmark (225)-issue Nikkei Stock Average rose (356.17) points, or (1.98)%, to close at (18,348.13).
   [日経225指標銘柄平均株価は、356.17ポイント（1.98%）上昇し、終値は18,348円13銭だった]

   benchmark 225-issue Nikkei Stock Average　日経225指標銘柄平均株価

200

3) Google share prices rose by (1.4)%, rising to $(374.77) {£(216)}, while Yahoo rose (1.5)% to $(31.93) {£(18.40)}.
   [グーグル株は、1.4%値上がりして 374.77 ドル（216 ポンド）になり、ヤフー株は 1.5%値上がりして、31.93 ドル（18.40 ポンド）となった]

4) The company's share price reportedly rose from (17) yuan a share in late (2002) to more than (80) yuan in February (2008).
   [その会社の株価は、2002 年後半の 1 株あたり 17 元から、2008 年 2 月には 80 元以上に値上がりしたようである]
   　　yuan　中国の通貨単位・元、ユアン

5) The gaming product company's share price surged on the news, rising (304) yen, or (17.1)%, to (2,085) yen on the Tokyo Stock Exchange.
   [ニュースを受けてそのゲーム制作会社の株価は急騰し、東京証券取引所で 304 円、17.1%値上がりして 2,085 円になった]

6) The benchmark Dow Jones Average plunged below (12,000) points with a tumble of (419.94) points {(3.47) percent} to (11,679.36) and the NASDAQ slumped (100.06) points {(4.28) percent} to (2,239.96).
   [ダウ＝ジョーンズ平均株価は、419.94 ポイント安（3.47%）で、11,679.36 になり、12,000 ポイント以下に急落した。ナスダックは、100.06 ポイント安（4.28%）で、2,239.96 だった]

🔘 2TRACK 38

2 CD から流れてくる日本語を聴き、即座に英語に直して発話してください。（＊日本語の後ポーズがあって、その後すぐに英語が流れます）

1)　　　　　　　　　　　　2)
3)　　　　　　　　　　　　4)
5)

解答

1) 40 億ドルの社債発行　　　　a four-billion-dollar bond issue
2) 時価総額 180 億ドル　　　　a market capitalization of $18 bn
3) 5 万カナダドル国債　　　　a 50,000-Canadian-dollar bond
4) 24 億ポンドの含み損　　　　paper loss of £2.4 bn

5) 株式投資における、4兆737億円の含み損
   a potential loss of ¥4.0737 trillion on their stock market investment

3 以下の日本語を英語に直して発話してください。　2TRACK 39

1) 日経平均は80ポイント、0.66%安で終えた。

2) 所有者は、その企業の株式50%を売却した。

3) 株は現在、4ドル強で取引されている。

4) 含み損は、143億9,400万円だった。

5) 1株の値段は220ドルで、その会社は3：1の株式分割を希望している。

解答

1) The Nikkei Stock Average closed down 80 points, or 0.66%.
2) The owner sold a 50% stake in the company's equity.
3) The shares are now trading at just over four dollars.
4) Unrealized losses were ¥14.394 billion.
5) One share cost $220 and the company wants to make a three-for-one share split.

34 売上げ、利益、損益（費用）・徹底トレーニング Step 2

📀 2TRACK 40

1 CDから流れてくる英文を聴き、カッコの部分を書き取ってください。

1) The (　　) quarter revenue was up (　　)% on the previous year to $(　　) bn, while its profits rose (　　)% to $(　　) bn.

2) India's biggest steel producer's domestic net profit declined to (　　) bn rupees {$(　　) m; £(　　) m} in the last (　　) months of (　　).

3) The German firm saw a net profit of €(　　) m {$(　　) m; £(　　) m} in the last (　　) months of (　　).

4) Their (　　) loss totaled $(　　) bn {£(　　) bn}, which is the biggest annual loss in U.K. corporate history.

5) Total sales increased by (　　)% to $(　　) bn, while net profits rose to $(　　) m from $(　　) m, year on year.

6) Their website said that in (　　), they had a turnover approaching $(　　) {£(　　)}.

解答

1) The (fourth) quarter revenue was up (17)% on the previous year to $(7.6) bn, while its profits rose (24)% to $(2.1) bn.
　　[第4四半期の売上げは、前年比17％増加の76億ドルで、収益は24％の増加で21億ドルとなった]

2) India's biggest steel producer's domestic net profit declined to (4.7) bn rupees {$(95) m; £(66) m} in the last (three) months of (2008).
　　[インド最大の鉄鋼メーカーは、国内純益が2008年最後の3ヵ月で、47億ルピー（9,500万ドル、6,600万ポンド）に減少した]

203

3) The German firm saw a net profit of €(120) m {$(155) m; £(79) m} in the last (three) months of (2007).
   [そのドイツの会社は、2007年最後の3ヵ月で1億2,000万ユーロ（1億5,500万ドル、7,900万ポンド）の純益を上げた]

4) Their (2008) loss totaled $(34.2) bn {£(24.1) bn}, which is the biggest annual loss in U.K. corporate history.
   [彼らの2008年の損失総額は、342億ドル（241億ポンド）となったが、これは年間の損失額としては英国企業史上最大である]

5) Total sales increased by (6.4)% to $(13.3) bn, while net profits rose to $(441) m from $(320) m, year on year.
   [前年比で、総売上げは6.4%増の133億ドルになり、純益は3億2,000万ドルから4億4,100万ドルに上昇した]

6) Their website said that in (2006), they had a turnover approaching $(102,733) {£(70,000)}.
   [彼らのウェブサイトによると、2006年は102,733ドル（70,000ポンド）近い総売上げを達成した]

2TRACK 41

2 CDから流れてくる日本語を聴き、即座に英語に直して発話してください。（＊日本語の後ポーズがあって、その後すぐに英語が流れます）

1)   2)
3)   4)
5)

解答

1) 1億7,000万ポンド以上の損失　　losses of more than £170 M
2) 純益9,320ドル　　a net profit of $9,320
3) 400億ドルの記録的な貿易黒字　　a record trade surplus of forty billion dollars
4) 5億ドル相当の武器の売上げ　　a sale of five hundred million dollars' worth of arms
5) グループの純損失：600億円　　Group net loss: ¥60 bn

3 以下の日本語を英語に直して発話してください。　🔊 2TRACK 42

1) 日本の1月の赤字は、3,480億円だった。

2) 彼らの年商は、3億ポンドを超えた。

3) 世界中の音楽の売上げは、320億ドルになった。

4) その会社は、20億ドルの利益を予測した。

5) 2007-08会計年度に1,420万ポンドの損失

解答

1) Japan had a ¥348 bn deficit in January.
2) They had annual sales in excess of £300 M.
3) Worldwide music sales amounted to $32 bn.
4) The company forecast a profit of two billion dollars.
5) a £14.2 m loss for the 2007/08 financial period

35 料金、価格・徹底トレーニング Step 2

1 CD から流れてくる英文を聴き、カッコの部分を書き取ってください。

1) K ( )-( ) Vacuum Cleaner: $( ) - $( ) at ( ) stores

2) The winning bids totaled $( ).

3) ( )-bedroom residences priced from $( ) to over $( )

4) Customs officials have seized ( ) kilograms of heroin with a street value of more than ( ) dollars.

5) Size: ( ) bedrooms, ( ) bath; Rent: $( ); Parking: outdoor, when available, $( ).

6) Gas station prices have soared above $( ) {£( )} a U.S. gallon {about ( ) of a U.K. gallon} in some areas.

7) We had to pay the higher tuition of £( ) a year and nearly £( ) for a student house.

解答

1) K (5912)-(900) Vacuum Cleaner: $(139.37) - $(169.96) at (3) stores
   [K5912-900 型電気掃除機：3 店舗の価格は 139 ドル 37 セント～169 ドル 96 セント]

2) The winning bids totaled $(19,592,420,000).
   [落札額は、合計 195 億 9,242 万ドルだった]

3) (Two-and three)-bedroom residences priced from $(1,300,000) to over $(3,000,000)
   [寝室が 2～3 部屋ある住宅で、価格は 130 万～300 万ドル超まで]

4) Customs officials have seized (40) kilograms of heroin with a street value of more than (800,000) dollars.
　　［税関職員は、末端価格 80 万ドル以上となる 40 キログラムのヘロインを押収した］

5) Size: (two) bedrooms, (one) bath; Rent: $(1,895); Parking: outdoor, when available, $(250).
　　［タイプ：2 ベッドルーム＋1 バスルーム、賃料：1,895 ドル、駐車場：戸外、空きがある場合、250 ドル］

6) Gas station prices have soared above $(2) {£(1.24)} a U.S. gallon {about (four-fifths) of a U.K. gallon} in some areas.
　　［スタンド価格は、地域によっては 1 米ガロン（英ガロンの 4/5 に相当）あたり 2 ドル（1.24 ポンド）以上に跳ね上がった］

7) We had to pay the higher tuition of £(3,070) a year and nearly £(4,000) for a student house.
　　［年間 3,070 ポンドに値上がりした授業料と、学生寮費の約 4,000 ポンドを、われわれは支払わなければならなかった］

🎧 2TRACK 44

2 CD から流れてくる日本語を聴き、即座に英語に直して発話してください。（＊日本語の後ポーズがあって、その後すぐに英語が流れます）

1)　　　　　　　　　　　2)
3)　　　　　　　　　　　4)
5)

解答

1) 1 泊 500 ドルのホテル代　　　　　　　　hotel rates of $500 a night
2) 税込みで年間 50 ドルの手数料
　　　　　　　　a commission of 50 dollars (tax included) per year
3) 電気代は 9%、ガス代は 7%の上昇
　　　　　　　　a 9% increase in electricity rates and a 7% rise in gas rates
4) 5〜8 ドルまでの、多くの食事オプション
　　　　　　　　　　　　　　many meal options between $5 and $8
5) 40 ポンドのコンピュータ配送料
　　　　　　　　　　　　　　a £40 delivery charge for the computer

3 以下の日本語を英語に直して発話してください。　　🎧 2TRACK 45

1) 彼女の抗がん剤治療費は、ひと月 4,000 〜 9,000 ドルかかった。

2) 3 品のコース料理 2 名分で、約 100 ユーロぐらいかかる。

3) 従業員は、給与から家賃 50 ポンド、交通費 20 ポンドが控除されていた。

4) 彼らは、ひと月 1,300 ドルの家賃の他に、倉庫代の 100 ドルを支払った。

5) その機械は、時価よりも 40 ポンド安い 159.99 ポンドになる。

[解答]

1) Her anti-cancer drug treatment cost between $4,000 and $9,000 a month.
2) A three-course meal for two costs about 100 euros.
3) The workers had £50 for rent and £20 for transport deducted from their wages.
4) They paid $1,300 a month plus an extra hundred for a storage space.
5) The machine will cost £159.99, £40 less than the current price.

36 収入、支出、税金・徹底トレーニング Step 2

1 CDから流れてくる英文を聴き、カッコの部分を書き取ってください。

1) A German MP receives a monthly salary of €(　　) {£(　　)}.

2) He has asked to be paid between (　　) to (　　) dollars monthly with a performance bonus in cash.

3) The politician attempted to reduce their allowance from £(　　) to £(　　).

4) Most students will need a minimum of US$(　　)-(　　) for food and miscellaneous expenses per term.

5) Moldova remains the poorest country in Europe, with an average monthly salary of just over (　　) Moldovan Lei {£(　　), $(　　)} at the end of (　　).

6) The average after-tax annual income for salaried employees in Japan in (　　) was (　　) yen for (　　) hours of work, or (　　) yen / hour.

7) The estimated cost of living in Japan for a period of one year is ¥(　　) or about U.S.$(　　)-(　　).

解答

1) A German MP receives a monthly salary of €(7,339) {£(6,740)}.
 ［ドイツの国会議員は、月給として7,339ユーロ（6,740ポンド）を、受け取っている］

2) He has asked to be paid between (8,000) to (10,000) dollars monthly with a performance bonus in cash.
 ［彼は、月額8,000～10,000ドルの現金での業績手当を、要求している］

3) The politician attempted to reduce their allowance from £(5,625) to £(4,500).
   [その政治家は、彼らの手当を 5,625 から 4,500 ポンドに減らすように企てた]

4) Most students will need a minimum of US$(1,500)-(2,000) for food and miscellaneous expenses per term.
   [ほとんどの学生が、食費とその他雑費として 1 学期あたり、最低 1,500 〜 2,000 米ドルを必要とする]

5) Moldova remains the poorest country in Europe, with an average monthly salary of just over (2,500) Moldovan Lei {£(167), $(243)} at the end of (2008).
   [モルドバはいまだにヨーロッパの最貧国であり、2008 年末の時点で、平均月収は 2,500 モルドバレイ（167 ポンド、243 ドル）を少し超える程度である]

   　　　　　Moldovan Leu　モルドバの通貨・レイ　　＊複数形は Lei

6) The average after-tax annual income for salaried employees in Japan in (2001) was (5,576,676) yen for (1,848) hours of work, or (3,018) yen / hour.
   [2001 年の日本の給与所得者の平均手取り年収は、1,848 時間労働に対して 557 万 6,676 円、すなわち、時給換算で 3,018 円だった]

7) The estimated cost of living in Japan for a period of one year is ¥(1,080,000) or about U.S.$(9,000)-(10,000).
   [日本に住む場合の年間推定生活費は、108 万円、約 9,000 〜 10,000 米ドルである]

🎧 2TRACK 47

2 CD から流れてくる日本語を聴き、即座に英語に直して発話してください。（＊日本語の後ポーズがあって、その後すぐに英語が流れます）

1)　　　　　　　　　　2)
3)　　　　　　　　　　4)
5)

解 答

1) 今週の交通費：159 ドル 18 セント　　Transportation expenditures for this week: $159.18
2) 最低賃金：時給 7 ドル 25 セント　　The minimum wage: $7.25 per hour
3) 月収 5,180 ユーロ　　a monthly salary of 5,180 euros
4) 契約ボーナス 100 万ドル　　a signing bonus of one million dollars
5) 手取り収入：165,971 円　　After-tax income: 165,971 yen

3　以下の日本語を英語に直して発話してください。　2TRACK 48

1) 平均的な学生は、生活費に週 253 ポンド使う。

2) 彼は月収 8,000 米ドルで、さらに車と住宅手当を支給されている。

3) 平均的な給与所得者だったら、翌年の所得税が 10% 低くなる。

4) 彼の週給は、税込みで 3 万 7,000 ポンドだった。

5) 食費を 590 ドル節約するための、簡単な 5 つのヒント

解 答

1) The average student spends £253 a week on living expenses.
2) He earns US$8,000 dollars per month, plus a car and housing allowance.
3) Average wage-earners would pay 10% less income tax next year.
4) His weekly salary was £37,000 pre-tax.
5) five easy tips to save $590 on your food budget

37 ローン、クレジット、金利・徹底トレーニング Step 2

1 CDから流れてくる英文を聴き、カッコの部分を書き取ってください。

1) The effects have also been felt by home owners with rate rises adding a total of around £(　　) a month to an average £(　　) mortgage.

2) The housing loan was for £(　　) (　　) years ago, and (　　) years ago we took out a home improvement loan of £(　　).

3) They signed previously agreed loans worth ¥(　　) bn {$(　　) m; £(　　) m} for (　　) economic projects.

4) The government loan of €(　　) m {$(　　) m; £(　　) m} to the airline company was the illegal state aid.

5) They estimated that eventually the bank could be forced to write off up to $(　　) million {¥(　　) million} in bad loans, roughly (　　) the losses it has acknowledged.

解答

1) The effects have also been felt by home owners with rate rises adding a total of around £(50) a month to an average £(60,000) mortgage.
　　[平均6万ポンドの住宅ローンに対し、ローン金利が毎月総額約50ポンド上昇するため、住宅保有者もまたその影響を実感している]

2) The housing loan was for £(27,500) (16) years ago and (six) years ago we took out a home improvement loan of £(9,000).
　　[住宅ローンは、16年前27,500ポンドだった。そして6年前、9,000ポンドで住宅の改装のための融資を受けた]

3) They signed previously agreed loans worth ¥(103) bn {$(862) m; £(444) m} for (four) economic projects.
　　[彼らは、以前合意に達した1,030億円（8億6,200万ドル、4億4,400万ポンド）相当の、4つの経済計画の借款契約にサインした]

4) The government loan of €(400) m {$(495) m; £(275) m} to the airline company was the illegal state aid.
   [その航空会社への4億ユーロ（4億9,500万ドル、2億7,500万ポンド）の政府融資は、国からの違法な援助であった]

5) They estimated that eventually the bank could be forced to write off up to $(10) million {¥(950) million} in bad loans, roughly (twice) the losses it has acknowledged.
   [彼らの予測は、その銀行は最終的に1,000万ドル（9億5,000万円）もの不良債権を、回収不能とせざるを得ないかもしれないというものだった。それは、銀行が認識している額のほぼ2倍の損失である]

🔘 2TRACK 50

2 CDから流れてくる日本語を聴き、即座に英語に直して発話してください。（＊日本語の後ポーズがあって、その後すぐに英語が流れます）

1)
2)
3)

解答

1) 頭金なしの3年ローン
   　　　　　　　　　　　　　a three-year loan with no initial down payment
2) 2国への10億ドルの融資
   　　　　　　　　　　　　　one-billion-dollar credit to the two countries
3) 5億5,000万ドルの、分割払い金を支払う。
   　　　　　　　　　　　　　Make an installment payment of $550 M.

3 以下の日本語を英語に直して発話してください。　🔘 2TRACK 51

1) 金利：信用度の高い顧客向け、9.99%の低金利より

2) 分割払い：48ヵ月間月々の支払い額は同じ

3) 新しい住宅ローン契約では、借り手に25%の頭金を求めている。

【解　答】
1) Interest rates: from as low as 9.99% to credit qualified customers
2) Installment Plan: equal monthly payments over 48 months
3) A new mortgage deal requires a 25% down payment from the borrower.

38 資産、貯蓄、負債・徹底トレーニング Step 2

1 CDから流れてくる英文を聴き、カッコの部分を書き取ってください。

1) Their debt has been reduced by almost £( ) m to £( ) m, for the ( ) months ending July ( ).

2) It sets new limits for cash withdrawals in dollars from $( ) to $( ) a month.

3) The only means of payment we accept is bank transfer. Fees : ¥( ), U.S.$( ) or Australian $( ).

4) Their combined assets amount to about $( ) bn {£( ) bn}—well ahead of the current leader, Deutsche Bank, which has assets of $( ) bn {£( ) bn}.

5) The ( )-year-old prime minister was born into a wealthy family, and his family has declared assets worth about ¥( ) million {$( ) million}.

解答

1) Their debt has been reduced by almost £(6) m to £(30.48) m, for the (12) months ending July (2008).
   [彼らの負債は、2008年7月末までの12ヵ月間で約600万ポンド減って、3,048万ポンドになった]

2) It sets new limits for cash withdrawals in dollars from $(250) to $(400) a month.
   [ドルによる新たな現金引き出し限度額は、1ヵ月250ドルから400ドルとなっている]

3) The only means of payment we accept is bank transfer. Fees: ¥(5,500), U.S.$(55.00) or Australian $(68.00).
   [受け付けている支払い方法は、銀行振り込みのみとなります。手数料：5,500円、55米ドル、68豪ドル]

4) Their combined assets amount to about $(1,300) bn {£(812) bn}— well ahead of the current leader, Deutsche Bank, which has assets of $(735) bn {£(460) bn}.

　　[彼らの総資産は、約1兆3,000億ドル（8,120億ポンド）で、現在業界を引っ張っているドイツ銀行の資産7,350億ドル（4,600億ポンド）よりもずっと多い]

5) The (68)-year-old prime minister was born into a wealthy family, and his family has declared assets worth about ¥(455) million {$(4.8) million}.

　　[68歳の首相は、裕福な家庭の生まれで、約4億5,500万円（480万ドル）の資産があると、彼の親族が公表している]

🔘 2TRACK 53

2 CDから流れてくる日本語を聴き、即座に英語に直して発話してください。（＊日本語の後ポーズがあって、その後すぐに英語が流れます）

1)　　　　　　　　　2)
3)

【解答】
1) 1,200万ポンドの価値の資産　　　property worth £12 M
2) 10兆ドルの預金　　　　　　　　ten trillion dollars of savings
3) 3,000万円にまでなる借金　　　　debt of up to ¥30 MM

3 以下の日本語を英語に直して発話してください。　🔘 2TRACK 54

1) マフィアは、その銀行を通して、200億ドルを資金洗浄しようとしていた。

2) 資産約5,500ドルが、行方がわからなくなっていると報道された。

3) 1人あたりの借金は、約670万円だ。

【解答】
1) The mafia was trying to launder $20 billion through the bank.
2) About $5,500 in property was reported missing.
3) The per capita debt is approximately ¥6.7 million.

39 保険、年金・徹底トレーニング Step 2

1 CDから流れてくる英文を聴き、カッコの部分を書き取ってください。

1) The firm's insurance premiums rose from (　　　) yen a year to (　　　) yen after the accident.

2) He was fined $(　　　) {£(　　　)} for failing to renew unemployment insurance.

3) She is being sued by her stepmother over a $(　　)-million {£(　　　)} -life insurance policy left by her father, who died in (　　　).

4) The policy will cover the insured person against accident or death when on duty for (　　　) rupees, around $(　　　).

5) The damage insurers put the bill from fire damage at about A$(　　) million {U.S.$(　　) million} — slightly less than the claims that resulted from Sydney's (　　) bush fires.

解 答

1) The firm's insurance premiums rose from (2,000,000) yen a year to (7,000,000) yen after the accident.
 [その会社の保険料は、事故を起こした後、年間200万から700万円に上がった]

2) He was fined $(169,000) {£(97,000)} for failing to renew unemployment insurance.
 [彼は、雇用保険を更新しなかったことで、16万9,000ドル（9万7,000ポンド）の罰金を科された]

3) She is being sued by her stepmother over a $(1)-million {£(650,000)} -life insurance policy left by her father, who died in (2008).
 [彼女は、2008年に亡くなった彼女の父親が遺した生命保検100万ドル（65万ポンド）をめぐって、継母から訴えられている]

4) The policy will cover the insured person against accident or death when on duty for (100,000) rupees, around $(2,000).
　　[その保険は、被保険者の仕事中の事故かまたは死亡に対して10万ルピー、約2,000ドルの補償をする]

5) The damage insurers put the bill from fire damage at about A$(50) million {U.S.$(25.52) million} — slightly less than the claims that resulted from Sydney's (1994) bush fires.
　　[損害保険会社は、火災被害に対して約5,000万豪ドル（2,552万米ドル）の明細書を出した—それは1994年のシドニーの山火事のときの支払い要求額より少し低かった]

🎵 2TRACK 56

2 CDから流れてくる日本語を聴き、即座に英語に直して発話してください。（＊日本語の後ポーズがあって、その後すぐに英語が流れます）

1)　　　　　　　　　　　　　2)
3)

解 答

1) 3,000万円の生命保険の支払い金
　　　　　　　a 30-million-yen payout on life insurance policies
2) 約10万ドルの年間保険料
　　　　　　　annual insurance premiums around $100,000
3) 合計40万ポンドにおよぶ、2つの保険証券
　　　　　　　two life insurance policies worth up to £400,000 in total

3 以下の日本語を英語に直して発話してください。　🎵 2TRACK 57

1) 彼の妹が、彼の100万ドルの生命保険金の受取人だ。

2) その損保会社は、損害賠償請求だけで2億ユーロに達すると見積もっている。

3) 日本郵政公社は、郵便貯金と簡易保険で、350兆円を保有する。

解 答

1) His sister is the beneficiary of his million-dollar life insurance policy.
2) The insurers estimate that damage claims alone will reach 200 million euros.
3) Japan Post has 350 trillion yen in postal savings and life insurance policies.

40 長さ、幅・徹底トレーニング Step 2

1 CDから流れてくる英文を聴き、カッコの部分を書き取ってください。

1) The playing area ranges from a minimum of (　　) m {(　　) yards} to a maximum of (　　) m {(　　) yards} long. Around this playing area is a safety zone, (　　) m {(　　) yards} wide along the sides and (　　) m {(　　) yards} deep.

2) The vessel was built in South Korea (　　) years ago and is (　　) m {(　　) yards} long and (　　) m {(　　) yards} wide.

3) Squash is played on an area (　　) ft {(　　) m} long by (　　) ft {(　　) m} wide for the (　　)-player game, and (　　) ft {(　　) m} wide for the (　　)-player game.

4) The ship was (　　) feet {(　　) m} long and (　　) feet {(　　) m} wide and had a draft of (　　) feet {(　　) m}.

5) The U.S.-Canadian border is nearly (　　) miles {(　　) km} long.

6) The area affected by the disaster is thought to be around (　　) km long and (　　) km wide.

解答

1) The playing area ranges from a minimum of (228.6) m {(250) yards} to a maximum of (274.2) m {(300) yards} long. Around this playing area is a safety zone, (9.15) m {(10) yards} wide along the sides and (27.45) m {(30) yards} deep.

　[競技場は、長さ最低228.6メートル（250ヤード）から、最大274.2メートル（300ヤード）にわたる。この競技場の周りはセイフティゾーンで、外周に沿って幅9.15メートル（10ヤード）、奥行き27.45メートル（30ヤード）である]

2) The vessel was built in South Korea (two) years ago and is (332) m {(363) yards} long and (58) m {(63) yards} wide.
   [その大型船は、2 年前に韓国で製造され、全長 332 メートル（363 ヤード）、全幅 58 メートル（63 ヤード）である］

3) Squash is played on an area (44) ft {(13.41) m} long by (17) ft {(5.18) m} wide for the (two)-player game, and (20) ft {(6.10) m} wide for the (four)-player game.
   [スカッシュは、シングルスの試合では、長さ 44 フィート（13.41 メートル）、幅 17 フィート（5.18 メートル）、ダブルスの試合では、幅 20 フィート（6.10 メートル）のコートでおこなわれる］

4) The ship was (1,031) feet {(314) m} long and (118.5) feet {(36) m} wide and had a draft of (38) feet {(11.6) m}.
   [その船は、全長 1,031 フィート（314 メートル）、全幅 118.5 フィート（36 メートル）で、喫水 38 フィート（11.6 メートル）であった］

5) The U.S.-Canadian border is nearly (5,592) miles {(9,000) km} long.
   [アメリカとカナダの国境線は、約 5,592 マイル（9,000 キロメートル）である］

6) The area affected by the disaster is thought to be around (12,000) km long and (150) km wide.
   [災害の影響を受けた範囲は、長さ約 12,000 キロメートル、幅 150 キロメートルと思われる］

🔊 2TRACK 59

2 CD から流れてくる日本語を聴き、即座に英語に直して発話してください。（＊日本語の後ポーズがあって、その後すぐに英語が流れます）

1)　　　　　　　　　　　2)
3)　　　　　　　　　　　4)
5)

解 答

1) 102 センチメートル 6 ミリメートル　　102 cm 6 mm
2) 10,000 マイル　　　　　　　　　　　10,000 miles
3) 6,100 キロメートル　　　　　　　　　6,100 km
4) 143 ヤード　　　　　　　　　　　　143 yards

| 5) | 1,800 フィート | 1,800 feet |

3 以下の日本語を英語に直して発話してください。　💿 2TRACK 60

1) 耐熱ボールは、直径 16 センチメートルだ。

2) （長さ）1,567 ヤードの鉄道トンネル

3) 湖は、長さ 90 マイル、最大幅は 2.5 マイルだ。

4) 1,620 キロメートルの海岸線

5) 22 口径のターゲットピストル

解答
1) The oven-proof bowl is 16 cm in diameter.
2) a 1,567-yard-long railway tunnel
3) The lake is 90 miles long and 2.5 miles at its widest point.
4) the 1,620-kilometer-long coastline
5) .22-caliber target pistols

41 体重、身長 / 体長・徹底トレーニング Step 2

🔘 2TRACK 61

1 CD から流れてくる英文を聴き、カッコの部分を書き取ってください。

1) He reckons that someone weighing (　　) kg will need to walk (　　) km to burn off a big dinner and someone weighing (　　) kg will need to walk (　　) km.

2) Their new baby weighed (　　) kg {(　　) lb (　　) oz} and measured (　　) cm {(　　) inches}.

3) Pilot whales grow up to (　　) meters {(　　) feet} long and weigh as much as (　　) kg {(　　) pounds}.

4) The male baby elephant, which weighed about (　　) kg {(　　) lbs}, took his first steps about (　　) minutes after his birth.

5) A man of (　　) {(　　) m} weighing (　　) kg {(　　) stone (　　) lb} has a BMI of (　　) / {(　　) × (　　)} ≒ (　　).

解答

1) He reckons that someone weighing (70) kg will need to walk (33) km to burn off a big dinner and someone weighing (100) kg will need to walk (23) km.

　　［ごちそう（での摂取カロリー）を燃焼するのに、体重 70 キログラムの人は 33 キロメートル歩く必要があり、100 キログラムの人は 23 キロメートル歩く必要があると彼は考えている］

2) Their new baby weighed (3.4) kg {(7) lb (7) oz} and measured (50.8) cm {(20) inches}.

　　［彼らの生まれたばかりの赤ちゃんは、体重 3.4 キログラム（7 ポンド 7 オンス）で、身長 50.8 センチメートル（20 インチ）だった］

　　oz = ounce　オンス　　＊ 1 oz = 1/16 pound ≒ 28g

3) Pilot whales grow up to (5) meters {(16) feet} long and weigh as much as (870) kg {(1,800) pounds}.
   [ごんどう鯨は、体長 5 メートル（16 フィート）、体重 870 キログラム（1,800 ポンド）にまで成長する]

4) The male baby elephant, which weighed about (140) kg {(308) lbs}, took his first steps about (15) minutes after his birth.
   [オスの赤ちゃん象は、体重約 140 キログラム（308 ポンド）で、生まれてから約 15 分後に歩き出した]

   lb = libra（ラテン語）　重さの単位、ポンドを表す記号。ポンドと読みます。

5) A man of (6'0") {(1.83) m} weighing (82) kg {(13) stone (1) lb} has a BMI of (82) / {(1.83) × (1.83)} ≒ (24).
   [身長 6 フィート（1.83 メートル）、体重 82 キログラム（13 ストーン 1 ポンド）の男性の BMI は、82 ÷（1.83 × 1.83）で約 24 になる]

   BMI = body-mass index　体格指標 = $\dfrac{体重}{身長 \times 身長}$

🔘 2TRACK 62

2 CD から流れてくる日本語を聴き、即座に英語に直して発話してください。（＊日本語の後ポーズがあって、その後すぐに英語が流れます）

1)　　　　　　　　　　　2)
3)

【解　答】
1)　5 フィート 3 インチ　　　　　five feet three inches、five foot three、five three
2)　3,600 グラム　　　　　　　　3,600 g
3)　159.8 センチメートル　　　　159.8 cm

3 以下の日本語を英語に直して発話してください。　🔘 2TRACK 63

1)　体重 35 ポンドの子ども

2)　身長 180 センチメートルの野球選手

3) 体重 50 キログラム以上の女性たち

[解 答]

1) a child weighing 35 pounds
2) the 180-centimeter-tall baseball player
3) women who weigh more than 50 kilograms

42 重さ・徹底トレーニング Step 2

1 CD から流れてくる英文を聴き、カッコの部分を書き取ってください。

1) Under his plan, people carrying up to (　　) grams {(　　) ounces} of opium, (　　) milligrams of heroin or (　　) milligrams of methamphetamine would face no criminal charges.

2) Florida is the largest producer in the U.S. with (　　　) tons forecast this year, followed by Louisiana with (　　　) tons.

3) The sandwich has (　　) calories and contains (　　) grams of fat, or (　　)% of the daily allowance, and (　　) milligrams of salt, which is (　　)% of the daily allowance.

4) In (　　) A.D. the Danes acquired (　　) kg of silver in return for going home. By (　　) A.D., payments to the Danes had increased to (　　) kg.

5) During last year's season, (　　) million kg tabacco was sold, itself a sharp fall from the record high of (　　) million kg sold in (　　).

解答

1) Under his plan, people carrying up to (2) grams {(0.07) ounces} of opium, (50) milligrams of heroin or (40) milligrams of methamphetamine would face no criminal charges.
　　[彼の案では、2 グラム（0.07 オンス）までのアヘン、50 ミリグラムまでのヘロインおよび 40 ミリグラムまでのメタンフェタミンの携帯は、刑事罰の適用を受けないことになる]

2) Florida is the largest producer in the U.S. with (15.8 million) tons forecast this year, followed by Louisiana with (11.3 million) tons.
　　[今年の収穫高で、フロリダがアメリカ国内で最大の 1,580 万トンを予測、ルイジアナが 1,130 万トンでそれに続いている]

3) The sandwich has (290) calories and contains (9) grams of fat, or (14)% of the daily allowance, and (680) milligrams of salt, which is (28)% of the daily allowance.

　　［このサンドイッチは 290 カロリーで、9 グラムの脂肪（1 日の摂取許容量の 14%）と 680 ミリグラムの塩分（1 日の摂取許容量の 28%）を含んでいる］

4) In (991) A.D. the Danes acquired (4,500) kg of silver in return for going home. By (1012) A.D., payments to the Danes had increased to (22,000) kg.

　　［紀元 991 年に、デーン人は（侵入をやめて）故郷へ帰る見返りに、4,500 キログラムの銀を入手した。1012 年までに、デーン人への支払いは、22,000 キログラムにまで増えた］

　　Dane　デーン人

　　＊デンマークの民族、イギリスでは Viking（バイキング）と呼ばれています。

5) During last year's season, (162) million kg tobacco was sold, itself a sharp fall from the record high of (237) million kg sold in (2000).

　　［去年のシーズン中、1 億 6,200 万キログラムのたばこが売れた。それ自体、2000 年の 2 億 3,700 万キログラムの記録的な販売量から激減だった］

🎧 2TRACK 65

2　CD から流れてくる日本語を聴き、即座に英語に直して発話してください。（＊日本語の後ポーズがあって、その後すぐに英語が流れます）

1)　　　　　　　　　　　2)
3)

解　答

1)	300 キログラム	300 kg
2)	140 ポンド	140 lb
3)	8 万トン	80,000 tons

3　以下の日本語を英語に直して発話してください。　🎧 2TRACK 66

1) 33 トンの国連救援物資を積んだ船

2) １キログラム（2.2 ポンド）のコカイン

3) １万グラムの金の延べ棒

解 答

1) a ship carrying 33 tons of U.N. aid
2) 1 kg or 2.2 lb of cocaine
3) 10,000 grams of gold bar

43 深さ / 奥行き、厚さ・徹底トレーニング Step 2

🎧 2TRACK 67

1 CDから流れてくる英文を聴き、カッコの部分を書き取ってください。

1) During the (　) days of the year when these waters are not covered by a layer of ice that is almost (　) meters thick, crews on the rig will have to battle with (　)-meter waves.

2) The fault is closest to the surface in the south — about (　) km {(　) miles} down — and reaches to a depth of about (　) km {(　) miles} towards the north.

3) The wrecked ship is thought to be more than (　) km {(　) miles} deep under notoriously rough seas, some (　) km {(　) miles} off the Argentine coast.

4) The gigantic island measures (　) million square kilometers {(　) square miles} — (　)% of it covered with ice that is up to (　) meters {(　)} feet thick.

5) It is (　) km long and up to (　) km deep in places, more than (　) times deeper than the Grand Canyon in Arizona.

解答

1) During the (110) days of the year when these waters are not covered by a layer of ice that is almost (two) meters thick, crews on the rig will have to battle with (12)-meter waves.
　　[1年のうち、この海域から約2メートルの厚さの氷の層が消える110日の間、掘削作業員たちは12メートルの波と闘わねばならないだろう]

2) The fault is closest to the surface in the south — about (3) km {(1.8) miles} down — and reaches to a depth of about (17) km {(10.5) miles} towards the north.
　　[その断層は、南部では地表に最も近く—深度約3キロメートル（1.8マイル）—北部へ行くと約17キロメートル（10.5マイル）の深さに達する]

3) The wrecked ship is thought to be more than (4) km {(2 1/2) miles} deep under notoriously rough seas, some (180) km {(112.5) miles} off the Argentine coast.
   [その難破船は、アルゼンチン沿岸から約180キロメートル（112.5マイル）離れた、悪名高い荒海の深さ4キロメートル（2.5マイル）以上のところに沈んでいると考えられている]

4) The gigantic island measures (2.2) million square kilometers {(844,000) square miles}—(85)% of it covered with ice that is up to (4,000) meters {(11,000)} feet thick.
   [その巨大な島は、面積220万平方キロメートル（84万4,000平方マイル）—その85%が、厚さ4,000メートルまでになる（1万1,000フィート）氷に覆われている]

5) It is (4,000) km long and up to (10) km deep in places, more than (six) times deeper than the Grand Canyon in Arizona.
   [それは長さ4,000キロメートル、場所によっては深さが10キロメートルにまでなり、アリゾナ州のグランドキャニオンの6倍以上の深さになる]

2TRACK 68

2 CDから流れてくる日本語を聴き、即座に英語に直して発話してください。（*日本語の後ポーズがあって、その後すぐに英語が流れます）

1)   2)
3)

解答

1) 深さ2,000フィート以上   depth of more than 2,000 feet
2) 厚さ350キロメートル   thickness of 350 km
3) 厚さ約1ミリメートル   approximately 1 mm in thickness

3 以下の日本語を英語に直して発話してください。 2TRACK 69

1) 厚さ5〜40キロメートルの氷殻

2) 30センチメートル四方で深さ6メートル

3) 厚さ2マイルの氷床

解答

1) between 5- and 40-kilometer-thick ice crust
2) 30 centimeters square by 6 meters deep
3) a two-mile-thick ice sheet

44 高さ、高度（標高、海抜）・徹底トレーニング Step 2

1 CD から流れてくる英文を聴き、カッコの部分を書き取ってください。

1) The meteors burn up at ( )-( ) miles {( )-( ) km} in altitude.

2) The route starts just ( ) m {( ) ft} above sea level, leaving about ( ) m {( ) ft} of ascent still to cover.

3) The plane was at an altitude of ( ) m {( ) ft}, but one of the plane's altimeters recorded an altitude of minus ( ) m {minus ( ) ft}.

4) Distance covered ( ) miles, top speed ( ) mph, total inclines ( ) feet, highest altitude ( ) feet.

5) Mount Kenya, an extinct volcano, has ( ) peaks: Batian at ( ) meters; Nelion at ( ) meters; and Point Lenana at ( ) meters.

解答

1) The meteors burn up at (60)-(75) miles {(100)-(120) km} in altitude.
   [隕石は、高度 60 ～ 75 マイル（100 ～ 120 キロメートル）で燃える]

2) The route starts just (57) m {(181) ft} above sea level, leaving about (850) m {(2,700) ft} of ascent still to cover.
   [ルートは、海抜 57 メートル（181 フィート）の地点から始まるが、さらに約 850 メートル（2,700 フィート）上がらねばならない]

3) The plane was at an altitude of (595) m {(1,950) ft}, but one of the plane's altimeters recorded an altitude of minus (2.4) m {minus (8) ft}.
   [飛行機は、高度 595 メートル（1,950 フィート）を飛行していたが、高度計の 1 つは高度マイナス 2.4 メートル（マイナス 8 フィート）を記録していた]

4) Distance covered (855) miles, top speed (47.5) mph, total inclines (57,000) feet, highest altitude (6,215) feet.
   [距離 855 マイル、最高時速 47.5 マイル、傾斜は合計 57,000 フィート、最高高度 6,215 フィート]

5) Mount Kenya, an extinct volcano, has (three) peaks: Batian at (5,147) meters; Nelion at (5,136) meters; and Point Lenana at (4,935) meters.
   [ケニヤ山は死火山で、ピークが3つある。バチアン（5,147メートル）、ネリオン（5,136メートル）、ポイントレナナ（4,935メートル）だ]

🎧 2TRACK 71

2 CDから流れてくる日本語を聴き、即座に英語に直して発話してください。（＊日本語の後ポーズがあって、その後すぐに英語が流れます）

1)　　　　　　　　　　　　2)
3)

解答

1) 最高高度 2.9 メートル　　　　maximum height 2.9 m
2) 最高高度 8,516 フィート　　　the highest altitude of 8,516 feet
3) 海抜 1,000 フィート　　　　　1,000 ft above sea level

3 以下の日本語を英語に直して発話してください。　🎧 2TRACK 72

1) スタジアムの高度は、海抜約 3,700 フィートだった。

2) 1万 8,500 フィートの地点付近での作業

3) 対角線：長さ 7.5 ミリメートル、高さ 0.85 ミリメートル

解答

1) The stadium's altitude was about 3,700 feet above sea level.
2) working at around the 18,500-foot mark
3) A diagonal line: a length of 7.5 mm and a height of 0.85 mm

45 面積、容積/体積・徹底トレーニング Step 2

1 CD から流れてくる英文を聴き、カッコの部分を書き取ってください。

1) (　　) MPG is equivalent to (　　) gallons per (　　) miles, and (　　) MPG translates into (　　) gallons per (　　) miles.

2) He wants to extract (　　　) tons of fluorite ore from a (　　　) -hectare {(　　)-acre} section of the quarry site.

3) An object exploded, flattening (　　　) trees over an area of (　　) square km {(　　) square miles}.

4) A volume of (　　　) cubic yards {(　　　) cubic meters} of material was removed.

5) Filled with (　　　) cubic meters {(　　) million cubic feet} of non-flammable helium, the airship will be (　　) meters {(　　) feet} long.

6) Wetlands that covered (　　) square km {(　　) square miles} in the early (　　) had dwindled to just (　　) square km {(　　) square miles} by (　　).

解答

1) (Eighteen) MPG is equivalent to (5.5) gallons per (100) miles, and (28) MPG translates into (3.6) gallons per (100) miles.
　　[18 mpg は 100 マイルあたり 5.5 ガロンに相当し、28 mpg は 100 マイルあたり 3.6 ガロンに相当する]
　　　MPG = mile per gallon

2) He wants to extract (660,000) tons of fluorite ore from a (10.37)-hectare {(25.6)-acre} section of the quarry site.
　　[彼は、採石場の 10.37 ヘクタール（25.6 エーカー）の場所から、ホタル石の原石を 66 万トン掘り出したいと思っている]

234

3) An object exploded, flattening (80 million) trees over an area of (2,000) square km {(800) square miles}.
   [ある物体が爆発し、面積 2,000 平方キロメートル（800 平方マイル）の範囲にある 8,000 万本の木をなぎ倒した]

4) A volume of (2,500,000) cubic yards {(1,912,500) cubic meters} of material was removed.
   [体積 250 万立方ヤード（191 万 2,500 立方メートル）の物質が取り除かれた]

5) Filled with (500,000) cubic meters {(17.6) million cubic feet} of non-flammable helium, the airship will be (260) meters {(850) feet} long.
   [不可燃性のヘリウム 50 万立方メートル（1,760 万立方フィート）で満たされた飛行船は、全長 260 メートル（850 フィート）になる]

6) Wetlands that covered (9,000) square km {(3,475) square miles} in the early (1970s) had dwindled to just (760) square km {(293) square miles} by (2002).
   [1970 年代初頭に 9,000 平方キロメートル（3,475 平方マイル）広がっていた湿地帯は、2002 年までにわずか 760 平方キロメートル（293 平方マイル）に減少した]

2TRACK 74

2 CD から流れてくる日本語を聴き、即座に英語に直して発話してください。（＊日本語の後ポーズがあって、その後すぐに英語が流れます）

1)
2)
3)
4)
5)

解答

1) 70 平方ミリメートル　　　　70 mm^2
2) 1,500 立方メートル　　　　1,500 cubic meters
3) 1,000 ガロン　　　　　　　1,000 gallons
4) 350 立方フィート　　　　　350 cubic feet
5) 600 パイント　　　　　　　600 pints

3 以下の日本語を英語に直して発話してください。　🎧 2TRACK 75

1) その滝には、1分間に3万5,000ガロンの水が流れる。

2) 35,000エーカー規模の操業

3) 空の5ガロンの石油ドラム缶

4) 200平方フィート以下の売り場面積

5) 400立方センチメートルの大きさの脳

解答

1) The falls flow at 35,000 gallons per minute.
2) a 35,000-acre operation
3) empty 5 gallon oil drums
4) less than 200 square feet of selling space
5) a brain size of 400 cubic centimeters

46 距離、速度、角度・徹底トレーニング Step 2

🎧 2TRACK 76

1 CDから流れてくる英文を聴き、カッコの部分を書き取ってください。

1) The new model is a (   )-door coupe with a V-(   ) engine and will be able to accelerate from (   )-(   ) mph in less than (   ) seconds and reach (   ) mph in less than (   ) seconds.

2) Hammer a (   )-m to (   )-m {(   )-ft to (   )-ft} stake into the soil at a (   )-degree angle.

3) Here a tornado with winds estimated at {(   ) mph (   ) km/h} tore a path of damage {(   ) miles (   ) km} long and half a mile wide.

4) A giant canyon system stretches over (   ) km {(   ) miles} along the equator with an average depth of (   ) km.

5) While light travels at (   ) kilometers per second, sound is much slower at around (   ) kilometers per hour.

6) He was flying between (   ) and (   ) m above the sea at speeds between (   ) and (   ) km/h.

解答

1) The new model is a (two)-door coupe with a V-(12) engine and will be able to accelerate from (0)-(60) mph in less than (five) seconds and reach (100) mph in less than (11) seconds.

　　[その新型モデルは、V-12 エンジン搭載の 2 ドアクーペで、5 秒以内に時速 0～60 マイルに加速でき、11 秒以内に時速 100 マイルに達する]

2) Hammer a (1)-m to (1.2)-m {(3.3)-ft to (3.9)-ft} stake into the soil at a (45)-degree angle.

　　[1～1.2 メートル（3.3～3.9 フィート）の杭を、45 度の角度で地面に打ち込む]

3) Here a tornado with winds estimated at {(157) mph (253) km/h} tore a path of damage {(12) miles (19) km} long and half a mile wide.

[ここでは、風速毎時157マイル（毎時253キロメートル）と見られる竜巻が、長さ12マイル（19キロメートル）、幅0.5マイルにわたって、道路を寸断した]

4) A giant canyon system stretches over (5,000) km {(3,100) miles} along the equator with an average depth of (six) km.

[巨大な峡谷が、赤道に沿って5,000キロメートル（3,100マイル）にわたって広がっている。平均の深さは、6キロメートルである]

5) While light travels at (300,000) kilometers per second, sound is much slower at around (1,200) kilometers per hour.

[光が秒速30万キロメートルで進むのに比べると、音は時速約1,200キロメートルと、かなり遅い]

6) He was flying between (58) and (483) m above the sea at speeds between (56) and (90) km/h.

[彼は、海上58〜483メートルを、時速56〜90キロメートルで飛行していた]

2TRACK 77

2 CDから流れてくる日本語を聴き、即座に英語に直して発話してください。（＊日本語の後ポーズがあって、その後すぐに英語が流れます）

1)　　　　　　　　　　2)
3)　　　　　　　　　　4)
5)

解答

1) 2,797メートル　　　　2,797 m
2) 1,600マイル　　　　　1,600 miles
3) 時速241キロメートル　241 km/h
4) 1分間に250語　　　　250 words / min
5) 時速105〜119マイルの間　between 105 and 119 mph

3 以下の日本語を英語に直して発話してください。　🎧 2TRACK 78

1) 州都マディソンの南 15 マイル

2) 海岸線から 8〜16 キロメートル以内にある低地住宅地

3) 秒速 25 メートルに達する突風

4) 1 秒間に 5,000 を超える携帯メール

5) 時速 75 キロメートルの飛行、海上 13 メートル

解　答

1) 15 miles south of the state capital, Madison
   　　　　　　　Madison　マディソン（米国ウィスコンシン州の州都）
2) residential areas on low ground within 8-16 km of the shoreline
3) gusts of up to 25 meters per second
4) more than 5,000 text messages per second
   　　　　　　text message　携帯メール＝テキスト形式のメールメッセージ
5) flying at 75 km/h, 13 meters above the water

47 緯度、経度・徹底トレーニング Step 2

2TRACK 79

1 CDから流れてくる英文を聴き、カッコの部分を書き取ってください。

1) The image was centered at (　　) degrees south latitude, (　　) degrees east longitude.

2) We are now at latitude (　　) degrees (　　) minutes north and longitude (　　) degrees (　　) minutes west.

3) The hill stands (　　) feet above sea level, at a latitude (　　) (　　) N, longitude (　　) (　　) W.

4) The star chart is designed for latitude (　　) degrees (　　) minutes north and longitude (　　) degrees (　　) minutes west.

5) A few photos from South Africa: (　　) (　　) (　　) south latitude, (　　) (　　) (　　) east longitude.

解答

1) The image was centered at (33.26) degrees south latitude, (145.47) degrees east longitude.
　　[その画像は、南緯33度26分、東経145度47分を中心に置いていた]

2) We are now at latitude (64) degrees (4) minutes north and longitude (139) degrees (26) minutes west.
　　[私たちは現在、北緯64度4分、西経139度26分のところにいる]

3) The hill stands (200) feet above sea level, at a latitude (51°) (30') N, longitude (3°) (10') W.
　　[その丘は、海抜200フィート、北緯51度30分、西経3度10分に位置している]

4) The star chart is designed for latitude (54) degrees (16) minutes north and longitude (0) degrees (25) minutes west.
　　[その星図は、北緯54度16分、西経0度25分に合わせてある]

5) A few photos from South Africa: (34°) (21') (24") south latitude, (18°) (29') (51") east longitude.
   ［南アフリカからの数枚の写真：南緯 34 度 21 分 24 秒、東経 18 度 29 分 51 秒］

2TRACK 80

2 CD から流れてくる日本語を聴き、即座に英語に直して発話してください。（＊日本語の後ポーズがあって、その後すぐに英語が流れます）

1)
2)
3)

解 答

1) 緯度 35 度 28 分   Latitude: 35.28
2) 経度 139 度 57 分   Longitude: 139.57
3) 緯度 25 度 24 分 19 秒   Latitude: 25°24'19"

3 以下の日本語を英語に直して発話してください。   2TRACK 81

1) 緯度：40 度 50 分、経度 3 度 58 分

2) 緯度：35 度 10 分、経度 70 度 6 分

3) 経度：0 度、23 分、36.8 秒、グリニッジ子午線西

解 答

1) Latitude: 40 degrees 50 minutes, Longitude: 3 degrees 58 minutes
2) Latitude: 35 degrees 10 minutes, Longitude: 70 degrees 6 minutes
3) Longitude: 00 degrees, 23 minutes, 36.8 seconds west of the Greenwich Meridian

48 気象・徹底トレーニング Step 2

🎵 2TRACK 82

1 CDから流れてくる英文を聴き、カッコの部分を書き取ってください。

1) Ike is a Category (　　) hurricane, with winds of up to (　　) km/h {(　　) mph}.

2) One of the largest earthquakes ever, with a magnitude of (　　), was in Chile in (　　). (　　) years later, there was another in Alaska, with a (　　) magnitude on the Richter scale.

3) Today: hot with the temperature approaching the record of (　　) set in (　　) with sunshine and patchy clouds. High: (　　) / (　　)

4) A figure of (　　) millibars {(　　) inches of mercury} was recorded on January (　　) (　　) in Siberia.

5) The temperature climbed from (　　) at the start of the race to the high (　　) while the elite runners were still on the course, before reaching (　　) late in the morning.

解答

1) Ike is a Category (Three) hurricane, with winds of up to (185) km/h {(115) mph}.
　　［アイクはカテゴリー3のハリケーンで、最大風速、時速185キロメートル（時速115マイル）の風を伴う］
　　　Ike　アイク（男性の名前）＝ハリケーンの名前
　　　＊アメリカでは、ハリケーンを人の名前で呼びます。

2) One of the largest earthquakes ever, with a magnitude of (9.5), was in Chile in (1960). (Four) years later, there was another in Alaska, with a (9.2) magnitude on the Richter scale.
　　［これまでの最大級の地震の1つは、チリで起こった1960年のマグニチュード9.5の地震だ。そして、もう1つ、4年後のアラスカで起こった9.2の地震がある］

242

3) Today: hot with the temperature approaching the record of (98) set in (1953) with sunshine and patchy clouds. High: (97°F) / (36°C)
   [本日：雲はあるものの、晴れて気温が上昇。1953 年の最高気温、(華氏) 98 度に迫る暑さになるもよう。最高気温：華氏 97 度 / 摂氏 36 度]

4) A figure of (1075.2) millibars {(31.75) inches of mercury} was recorded on January (14) (1893) in Siberia.
   [1075.2 ミリバール（水銀柱 31.75 インチ）の数値が、1893 年 1 月 14 日にシベリアで記録された]

5) The temperature climbed from (65) at the start of the race to the high (70s) while the elite runners were still on the course, before reaching (84) late in the morning.
   [気温は、レーススタート時の 65 度から、有力選手の競技中に 70 度台後半まで上がり、正午近くには 84 度に達した]

🎧 2TRACK 83

2 CD から流れてくる日本語を聴き、即座に英語に直して発話してください。(＊日本語の後ポーズがあって、その後すぐに英語が流れます)

1)　　　　　　　　　　　　2)
3)

解 答

1) 摂氏 32 度、60%の湿度　　　　　　　32°C and 60% humidity
2) 雷を伴う雨の確率 80%　　　　　　　80% chance of rain with thunder
3) 風速は、時速 100 メートルを超えた。
　　　　　　　　　　　　　　Wind speeds topped 100 meters per hour.

3 以下の日本語を英語に直して発話してください。　🎧 2TRACK 84

1) 湿度 42%、気圧 1,011 ミリバール、上昇中

2) 曇り、摂氏 22 度、西の風（時速 15 キロメートル）

3) 気温の範囲は、華氏 62 度から 76 度

> 解 答

1) Humidity (%): 42　Pressure (mb): 1,011　Rising
   mb = millibar
2) Cloudy, 22°C, wind west (15 kilometers per hour)
3) a range of temperatures from 62°F to 76°F

付録 1

四則演算　Mathematical Equations

足し算　Addition　　$A + B = C$

☐ $4 + 6 = 10$　　(four plus six equals / is ten)

引き算　Subtraction　　$A - B = C$

☐ $9 - 2 = 7$　　(nine minus two equals / is seven、
　　　　　　　　 nine take away two equals / is seven、
　　　　　　　　 two from nine equals / is seven)

☐ $3 - 4.5 = -1.5$
　　　　(three minus four point five equals / is negative one point five、
　　　　 three minus four point five equals / is minus one point five)

掛け算　Multiplication　　$A \times B = C$

☐ $2 \times 3 = 6$　　(two times three equals / is six、
　　　　　　　　　 two multiplied by three equals / is six)

割り算　Division　　$A \div B = C$

☐ $28 \div 7 = 4$　　(twenty-eight divided by seven equals / is four、
　　　　　　　　　 seven goes into twenty-eight four times)

☐ $10 \div 3 = 3$ r 1
　　　　(ten divided by three equals / is three with a remainder of one)
　　　＊割り切れないときは、このように「r」を使う表現もあります。「r」は remainder（余り）の略です。

数学記号　Mathematical Symbols

- A > B　　　　　（A is greater than B）
- A < B　　　　　（A is less than B）
- A ≧ B　　　　　（A is greater than or equal to B）
- A ≦ B　　　　　（A is less than or equal to B）
- A ≒ B、A ≈ B　（A is approximately equal to B、
　　　　　　　　　A is approximately B）
- A ≠ B　　　　　（A is not equal to B）

概数を出す　Approximate Figures

切り上げる　round up

- round up to the nearest 100 yen
  [100円未満を、切り上げる]
- If 1.6 is rounded up to the nearest whole number, it becomes 2.
  [1.6（の小数点以下第1位）を、切り上げると2になる]
- Amounts are rounded up to the nearest dollar.
  [1ドル未満は、切り上げられます]

切り捨てる　round down、omit、drop

- round down / omit / drop the figures after the decimal point
  [小数点以下を、切り捨てる]
- If 5.3 is rounded down to the nearest whole number, it becomes 5.
  [5.3（の小数点以下第1位）を、切り捨てると5になる]

四捨五入する　round off

- round off ～ to the nearest whole number
  [～を、小数点以下第1位で四捨五入する]
- round off ～ to the nearest 100 dollars
  [～を、100ドル未満で四捨五入する]

☐ If 34.251 is rounded off to the second decimal place, it becomes 34.25.
  [34.251 が、小数点以下第 3 位で四捨五入されると、34.25 になる]

累乗	power

☐ X^2 (X squared)、X^3 (X cubed)、X^n (X to the nth (power))

付録2

換算演習問題　Conversion Practice

ほとんどのヨーロッパの国々では、日本と同じようにメートル法を使っていますが、イギリスやアメリカのようにヤード・ポンド法を使っている国もたくさんあります。頭の中ですばやく換算するためには、練習と慣れが必要です。

以下、換算式をもとに換算してみましょう。

1　What is 70 degrees Fahrenheit in Celsius?
　　[華氏70度は、摂氏何度ですか]
　　　＊ $(°F - 32) \times \dfrac{5}{9} = °C$

2　How tall is 160 cm in feet and inches?
　　[160センチメートルは、何フィート何インチですか]
　　　＊ 1 foot = 12 inches = 30.48 cm　　1 inch = 2.54 cm

3　How fast is 150 km/h in miles per hour?
　　[時速150キロメートルは、時速何マイルですか]
　　　＊ 1 mile ≒ 1.6 km

|解答・解説|

1　It's about 21 degrees Celsius.
　　[摂氏約21度]

　　　＊換算式は、$(°F - 32) \times \dfrac{5}{9} = °C$ ですが、$\dfrac{5}{9}$ が計算しにくい場合は、次の式を使って換算できます。$(°F - 32) ÷ 2 + \{(°F - 32) ÷ 2 \times 10\%\} = °C$
　　　　→ $(70 - 32) ÷ 2 = 19$
　　　　→ $19 + 1.9 ≒ 21$
　　　＊ °F ÷ 2 − 15 = °C でもほぼ同じ値が出ます。
　　　　→ $70 ÷ 2 − 15 = 20$
　　　＊「32°F = 0°C」、「平均体温は約98°F」と覚えておくと、便利です。

2 It's about 5'3".
　　［約 5 フィート 3 インチ］

　　　　＊ 1 フィート（フット）は、12 インチです。　まずインチに換算します。
　　　　＊ 1 インチ 2.5 センチメートルで計算すると、160 ÷ 2.5 = 64
　　　　　→ 64 インチをフィートに直します。64 ÷ 12 ≒ 5.3

3 It's about 94 mph.
　　［時速約 94 マイル］

　　　　＊ mph = miles per hour
　　　　＊ 150 ÷ 1.6 = 93.75 ≒ 94
　　　　＊ マイルからキロメートルに換算するときは、マイルにその数の半分を加えて、
　　　　　もとの数の 10%加えるとおおよその値が出ます。
　　　　　→ 94 + 47 + 9.4 = 150.4 ≒ 150

付録 3

チップの計算方法　Tip Calculation Method

チップの支払いで難しいのは、レストランやバー、タクシーでの会計時です。チップは、通常、代金の 15 〜 20％で、自分で計算し、なおかつそれを代金に加算して支払わなければなりません。

以下の問題を解いてみましょう。

☐ What is the tip on a $7.50 taxi fare? And how much do you need to pay in total?
　［7 ドル 50 セントのタクシー料金だと、チップはいくらですか。そして、合計でいくら支払えばいいでしょうか］

解答・解説

☐ It's about $1.50, so $9 total should be enough.
　［(チップを 20％とすると) 1 ドル 50 セントになり、(料金が 7 ドル 50 セントなので) 合計 9 ドルで十分です］

* チップを 20％で計算すると、7.50 × 0.2 = 1.5
　ちなみに 15％で計算すると、7.50 × 0.15 = 1.125
* 通常、10 ドル以下の代金に対しては、1 〜 2 ドルをチップとすれば問題ありません。
* 10 ドル以上 100 ドル未満の場合、合計金額の上 1 桁を 2 倍にします。例えば、50 ドルの場合、10 ドルがチップ、79 ドルの場合、14 ドルか 15 ドルがチップになります。
* また、100 ドル以上〜 1,000 ドル未満なら、合計金額の上 2 桁を 2 倍にします。100 ドルなら 20 ドルがチップ、410 ドルなら 82 ドルがチップになります。

著者略歴

大島さくら子（おおしま・さくらこ）

英語講師／通訳／語学カウンセラー
株式会社オフィス・ビー・アイ代表取締役
キャプラン・JALアカデミー・教育事業部、早稲田大学・エクステンションセンター、港区国際交流協会など、各種企業や団体で「ビジネス英会話」「英文ビジネスeメール」「ボランティア通訳養成」「TOEIC対策」など、さまざまな英語講座、セミナー、講演を担当。東京在住。
学歴：
・学習院女子短期大学（現：学習院女子大学、準学士）卒
・Temple University Japan（教養学部・アジア学専攻、学士）卒
・Oxford University（1 academic year）留学
出版：
「絶対に使える英文eメール作成術」（角川SSC新書）、「CD BOOK 実践ビジネス英会話」「CD BOOK 中級からの英文法」（共にべレ出版）、「正統派のTOEIC」（『週刊ST』コラム1997-2002連載、ジャパンタイムズ社）
資格：英検1級、TOEIC (R) 990

【英文校正／監修】

Allison Markin Powell

日本語翻訳家／編集者
10年間出版社に勤務後、現在、小説、エッセイ、ノンフィクション、漫画など様々なジャンルを扱うフリーの翻訳家／編集者として活躍中。ニューヨーク在住。
学歴：
・Dartmouth College（比較文学専攻、学士）卒
・Stanford University（日本現代文学専攻、修士）卒

CD BOOK 数量表現の英語トレーニングブック

2009年10月25日	初版発行
2012年 3月20日	第4刷発行
著者	大島 さくら子
カバーデザイン	赤谷直宣
カバーイラスト	桑原 節

©Sakurako Oshima 2009. Printed in Japan

発行者	内田 眞吾
発行・発売	べレ出版 〒162-0832 東京都新宿区岩戸町12 レベッカビル TEL (03) 5225-4790 FAX (03) 5225-4795 ホームページ http://www.beret.co.jp/ 振替 00180-7-104058
印刷	株式会社 文昇堂
製本	根本製本株式会社

落丁本・乱丁本は小社編集部あてにお送りください。送料小社負担にてお取り替えします。

ISBN 978-4-86064-243-3 C2082　　　　編集担当　脇山和美

英文校正 / 監修：

Allison Markin Powell

執筆協力：

伊藤寿子、宮本祥子

英文 / 和文校正：

渡辺則彰、戸室真希、岩澤明美、鈴木真紀子、峯祥一

英文校正：

Rike Wootten、Liam Sage

CDの内容　●時間…CD1（56分57秒）CD2（73分01秒）
　　　　　●ナレーション…Carolyn Miller・Chris Koprowski・久末絹代
　　　　　●収録内容：全ての徹底トレーニング

ビジネス英会話 パーフェクトブック

浅見ベートーベン 著

四六並製／定価 2730 円（5% 税込）本体 2600 円
ISBN978-4-86064-073-6 C2082　■ 432 頁

挨拶や訪問の時の会話から、交渉・プレゼンテーション、海外出張に必要なフレーズまで、あらゆるビジネスシーンを想定し、会社に必要な英語表現 4650 フレーズを 1 冊まとめました。一つ一つのフレーズは短くシンプルで、応用のきくものばかりなので、覚えやすく、すぐに使えます。CD 3 枚にすべてのフレーズを収録！

場面別 ビジネスマンのための英語表現集

関野孝雄 著

A5 並製／定価 2205 円（5% 税込）本体 2100 円
ISBN978-4-86064-149-8 C2082　■ 248 頁

外国人のお客様のお世話をするとき、海外出張に行くことになったときに役立つ表現集です。電話での応対、道案内、お客様を出迎えるとき、見送るとき、食事のとき、ミーティングの合間、電車などの移動中、などなど、実は一番会話に困る場面、状況で使える表現が満載です。外国人のお客様をアテンドすることになったときに必携の 1 冊です。

シーン別 本当に使える実践ビジネス英会話

大島さくら子／スティーブ・バーンスティン 著

A5 並製／定価 1995 円（5% 税込）本体 1900 円
ISBN978-4-86064-180-1 C2082　■ 280 頁

本書のダイアローグとその他の表現は、今、現場でばりばり働く"本物"のビジネスパーソンが使っている言葉だけで作成しています。つまり、日本人のための英語ではなく、ビジネス場面でネイティブ同士が、実際に使っている自然な生きた英語なのです。ビジネスシーンから仕事を離れた話題までのダイアローグを CD に収録。各場面ごとに表現のバリエーション・丁寧表現・カジュアル表現を紹介しています。

ビジネスミーティング すぐに使える英語表現集

関野孝雄 著

A5 並製／定価 2310 円（5% 税込） 本体 2200 円
ISBN978-4-86064-205-1 C2082 ■ 272 頁

長年、海外業務に携わってきた経験を持つ著者が書いた、ミーティングで本当に役立つ表現集。ミーティングの流れに沿って、進行役と参加者が使える表現をバリエーション豊富に紹介。マイクのチェックから、始まりの挨拶、ミーティングの主旨説明、お客様の紹介、自己紹介、プレゼン、質疑応答、討議、休憩、採決、終了の挨拶まで、細やかな場面もしっかりカバーした使える一冊。

CD-ROM 付き 英文ビジネスレター 実用フォーマットと例文集

高島康司 著

A5 並製／定価 1995 円（5% 税込） 本体 1900 円
ISBN978-4-939076-25-1 C2082 ■ 528 頁

さまざまなケースに使える豊富な実用フォーマットと、組み合わせが自由自在のたくさんの文例で、さまざまな用件に対応したビジネスレターが、すぐに正確に書くことができます。本の内容を素早く検索でき、フォーマットと例文をコピーして使える CD-ROM が付いて、時間短縮に役立てられます。

ビジネスですぐに使える Eメール英語表現集

ディー・オー・エム・フロンティア／味園真紀／小林知子 著

A5 並製／定価 1680 円（5% 税込） 本体 1600 円
ISBN978-4-86064-034-7 C2082 ■ 296 頁

海外とのビジネス、仕事上の連絡・つきあいに E メールは欠かせません。本書は、現場で日常的にメールで仕事をしているビジネスパーソンが作った使える英語表現集です。ビジネスシーンごとに項目を分け、実際のサンプルを紹介したうえで、そのシーンでよく使う単語・熟語をあげ、また組み合わせて使える応用表現を数多く紹介しています。簡単・簡潔な英文なのでそのままでも、または組み合わせても自由自在に使えます。

CD-ROM付き 英文社内メール すぐに使える例文集

高島康司／福岡洋子 著

A5 並製／定価 1995 円（5% 税込） 本体 1900 円
ISBN978-4-86064-174-0 C2082　■ 320 頁

社内や本社との連絡、報告などスピーディにこなしたいメール表現を豊富に収録。ミーティングやプレゼンテーション、提出書類やスケジュール、出勤日や休み、経理関係など社内業務の連絡、報告、人事や組織変更に関する連絡、在庫関連、出荷関連など営業に関する連絡と報告など、そのほかにも細かい用件に対応した表現を紹介していきます。本書の内容そのままをデータ化したCD-ROM付きです。

英文履歴書の書き方と実例集

田上達夫 著

A5 並製／定価 1995 円（5% 税込） 本体 1900 円
ISBN978-4-939076-94-7 C2082　■ 308 頁

レジュメ(職務経歴書)とカバーレター(自己PRするための文書)の実例を豊富に収録してあります。良い履歴書とは？　採用される履歴書とは？　を英文履歴書のプロが徹底的に追求して書いた本です。様々な職種に対応した本当にたくさんの実例は類書にはない充実度です。必ず採用になるポイントをきっちりおさえた履歴書の書き方を教授します。

CD BOOK 採用される英語面接 対策と実例集

田上達夫 著

A5 並製／定価 2100 円（5% 税込） 本体 2000 円
ISBN978-4-86064-049-1 C2082　■ 272 頁

さまざまな職種、経歴に対応した英語面接の質問・回答を豊富に収録してあります。言い直しのできないインタビューで、学歴や知識などの能力に加え、人間性、仕事への意欲など総合的な能力について、いかに面接官によい印象をあたえるか、その詳しい対策と回答例を紹介します。英語面接への不安を取り除き自信を持って望めるようになる本です。

英語プレゼンテーション すぐに使える技術と表現

妻鳥千鶴子 著

A5 並製／定価 2415 円（5% 税込） 本体 2300 円
ISBN978-4-86064-069-9 C2082　■ 368 頁

日本社会の国際化に伴い、日本人が英語で発表、英語で説明、英語でプレゼンテーションをする機会が増えています。本書は英語でプレゼンテーションをするときに必要な技術とよく使われる表現 3000 をまとめています。プレゼン原稿のアウトラインの作り方から効果的な発表の仕方までをやさしく解説。日本語表現から引ける索引付き。

MBA ENGLISH 経済・会計・財務の知識と英語を身につける

内之倉礼子 著

A5 並製／定価 2415 円（5% 税込） 本体 2300 円
ISBN978-4-86064-105-4 C2082　■ 352 頁

北米における〈会社の仕組み〉〈経済の仕組み〉の解説から、〈財務諸表と会社責任・企業統治〉〈貸借対照表・損益計算書・キャッシュフロー計算書〉そして〈財務諸表分析〉までの会計・財務の知識と英語を、実際にカナダで実務に携わる著者がわかりやすく解説する本書。MBA 取得を視野に入れた人も、ビジネスでこうした知識が必要な人も、まさに必携の 1 冊です。

MBA ENGLISH 経営・マーケティングの知識と英語を身につける

内之倉礼子 著

A5 並製／定価 2415 円（5% 税込） 本体 2300 円
ISBN978-4-86064-150-4 C2082　■ 360 頁

『MBA ENGLISH　経済・会計・財務の知識と英語を身につける』の姉妹編です。本書では前作であまり詳しく触れられなかった［経営・マーケティング］について詳しく学びます。前作とあわせれば MBA 取得に必要な基礎知識と英単語を身につけると同時に、MBA 留学で学ぶカリキュラムを疑似体験できます。